Whose Unconscious Is It?
Or,
A Deconstruction of Psychoanalysis and Neuropsychoanalysis
(2nd Edition)

by Adeeb Kasem

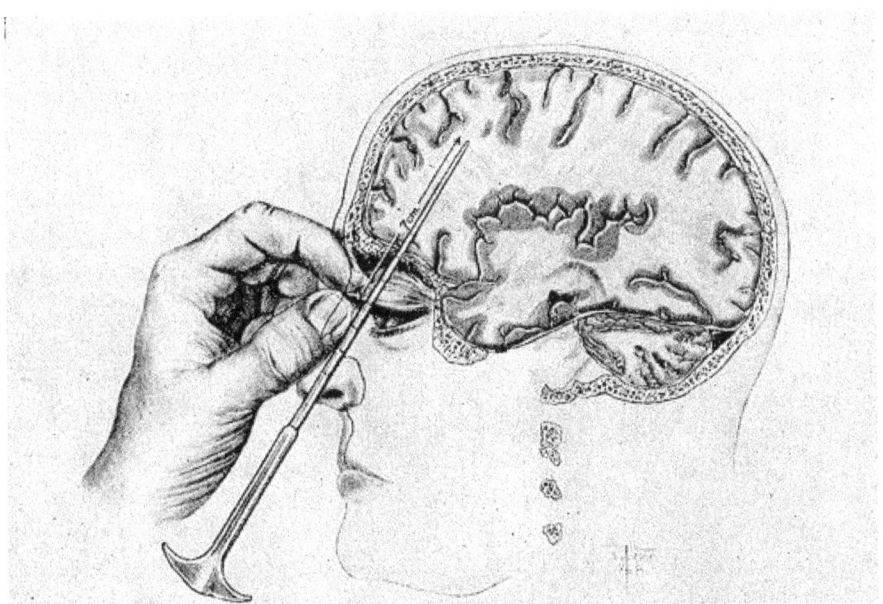

"Diagrammatic representation of trans-orbital lobotomy" from the manuscript for
Walter Freeman and James Watts' second edition of Psychosurgery (1950)

" I. *Materialism*

I.1 We shall now explain the principles.

I.2 Earth, water, fire and air are the principles, nothing else.

I.3 Their combination is called the "body", "sense" and "object".

I.4 Consciousness arises or is manifested out of these.

I.5 As the power of intoxication arises or is manifested from the constituent parts of the wine (such as flour, water and molasses).

I.6 The self is nothing but the body endowed with consciousness.

I.7 From the body itself.

I.8 Because of the existence of consciousness where there is a body.

I.9 Souls are like water bubbles."

—Carvaka aphorisms, adapted from the translation by Bhattacharya, "Carvaka Fragments: A New Collection"

"If Heaven I cannot bend, then Hell I will raise."
—Virgil, *Aeneid*

Table of Contents

Introduction: The Anals of Psychoanalysis

We do not pretend that this work is a thorough or comprehensive critique of psychoanalysis or its relation to the history of ideas; other authors have written much more comprehensive and scholarly works critiquing Freud and psychoanalysis, such as *Freud, Biologist of the Mind* by Frank Sulloway (1979), *The Discovery of the Unconscious: The History and Evolution of Dynamic Psychiatry* by Henri F. Ellenberger (1970), *Decline and Fall of the Freudian Empire* Hans Eysenck (1985), *Why Freud Was Wrong: Sin, Science and Psychoanalysis* by Richard Webster (1995), *Freud Evaluated: The Completed Arc* by Malcolm Macmillan (1991/1997), *Resistances of Psychoanalysis* by Jacques Derrida (1998), and *Anti-Oedipus* by Gilles Deleuze and Félix Guattari (1972/1977). For a critique of the institution of psychiatry itself, we refer the reader to Michel Foucault's *History of Madness* (1961/2006). These other authors often point out, as we do, that psychoanalysis is theological, pseudoscientific, and a means of control. In that respect, we have not presented a new thesis. Nor do we claim to have synthesized the critiques of others. We present here in this section another old thesis of theirs: Freud never cured anybody, and his most famous cases were failures which he fraudulently presented as miraculous successes.

The sociological conclusion is obvious: the myth of Freud as a "master" or "founding father" of psychology, cultivated by his "successes", makes of Freud a sage, genius, or culture hero and legitimates psychoanalysis and the bourgeois attitudes and beliefs which it upholds and propagates.

Almost as grievous a crime as teaching Freud in the classroom as a founding father of psychology is the habit of academics in the humanities to teach psychoanalysis as a valid method of literary or philosophical textual analysis, and to produce works which employ psychoanalysis. Psychoanalysis is a pseudoscience—if it can neither help patients nor give an insight into the mind, then it cannot have any validity as a method of interpretation. One may as well give a text an astrological or theological reading if one is giving it a psychoanalytic one. Psychoanalysis cannot reveal anything about a text because it assigns false causes to phenomena. For the same reason that the concept of race is no longer acceptable in discourse, neither should psychoanalysis be acceptable: they are superstitions and ideologies which promote oppression, and they are without a biological basis.

We will in detail refute Freud's theory of mind using as evidence facts from neuroscience, molecular biology, anthropology, and evolutionary biology. In addition, we will give a preliminary socioanalysis of Freud's ideas, demonstrating the functions they serve in a capitalist society. Our theoretical considerations are supported by examining Freud's "successful" cases, which scholars have demonstrated have been failures—failures of theory produce failures of practice.

Take for example, Little Hans:

"Another of Freud's key cases was that of "Little Hans," a 5-year-old boy who feared horses. According to Freud, the phobia originated in a fear of castration..."Little Hans" was Herbert Graf, the son of Max Graf, a Viennese musicologist who treated the boy under Freud's guidance...According to still unpublished finding by Mr. Stadlen, who has interviewed people who knew Herbert Graf, "the most straightforward explanation of his horse phobia" comes from Little Hans himself. "He said it started when he was frightened by horses at Gmunden, where he used to spend his summers," Mr. Stadlen said. He continued: "Freud discounts that as a cause of his phobia. But according to the members of the family with whom he stayed, it's very likely he, a visitor from the city, was warned that the horses could bite; bite they could."" (Goleman, 1990)

Little Hans was afraid that horses would bite him. Freud interpreted this, predictably, as a family problem: the horse is the father, and the biting is castration. He thus applies his easy formula, with no need to pay attention to the patient since the patient's explanation would merely be "resistance"—unless, of course, the patient provides the correct answer, which is always Oedipus. Little Hans is an innocent victim of psychoanalysis—he had a fear of horses, but Freud did not listen and instead made him out to be a naughty little boy who wants to fuck his mother and kill his father. Other misrepresented cases include Dora and the Wolf Man, which Freud also fraudulently maintained were miraculous successes (Goleman, 1990; Obholzer, 1982). The Wolf Man was never cured, and received treatment for the rest of his life (Goleman, 1990; Obholzer, 1982). For a discussion of Freud's failure to recognize that the Wolf Man's dream contained a multiplicity of wolves—as opposed to a single wolf which Freud predictably reduced to the Father—we refer the reader to Deleuze and Guattari's essay "One or Several Wolves?" contained in their book *A Thousand Plateaus* (1980/1987).

The founder of psychoanalysis never cured anybody—how is it possible that anyone following his methods and his theories, or methods and theories derived from his methods and theories, could ever cure anyone themselves? We argue that it is not possible, and that anyone who has claimed to be "cured" by psychoanalysis has been "cured" the same way that they could have been "cured" by a preacher or a folk healer—by magic, which is to say, by illusion, and that their problems were not real problems to begin with, but illusory problems.

Nortje et al. (2016), in their systematic review of published literature on the effectiveness of traditional healers in treating mental disorders compared with Western psychotherapy, conclude that:

"...many people, especially those with less severe complaints and positive expectations, derive subjective benefit from attending their chosen traditional or spiritual healers. Value seems to exist in attending a traditional healer for those who choose to do so and who find the process meaningful. This benefit might occur without a concomitant improvement in symptoms. The effective component of healing is often unclear, although intensive regular social interventions generally achieve superior outcomes to brief single interventions. That said, little evidence is available to suggest that traditional healers are effective in changing the course of major psychiatric illnesses such as schizophrenia or obsessive-compulsive disorder. Additionally, harms could be associated with traditional healing which we have not reviewed here." (p. 167)

The above quoted conclusion of Nortje et al. (2016) applies equally well to psychoanalysis—for those who believe in the religion, it may be perceived to be of benefit, but without a concomitant improvement in symptoms, and it cannot treat serious problems at all. Additionally, more harm may be done than good.

Analysts often stress the importance of "regular social interventions", i.e., regular sessions, over "brief single interventions", perhaps for the same reason that regular sessions are more effective in traditional healing: the "healer" builds more rapport with the patient and thereby the patient's *faith* in the healer increases. But faith is not medicine.

Countless studies exist promoting what is known as the Dodo Bird hypothesis, the hypothesis that all psychotherapies are equally effective—but the vast majority of these studies are undertaken by professionals who desire to preserve both their paychecks and their beliefs. If indeed the Dodo Bird hypothesis is true and all psychotherapies are equally effective, it also means that all psychotherapies are equally ineffective—that they are no better than witchcraft and that none of them really cure anyone. All psychiatry is just psychoanalysis in one form or another; drug-based psychiatry is a molecular psychoanalysis which aims to oedipalize the patient at the molecular level (Guattari, 1996, p. 153-154).

Pharmaceutical psychiatry, or drug-based psychiatry, is also just magic—drug-based traditional healing exists, and depending on the "illness" and the chemical, drug-based traditional healing may be more effective. For example, ibogaine, often used for religious purposes by the Bwiti religion of Africa, is exponentially more effective in treating drug addiction and alcoholism than all existing and prior treatments proffered by Western psychiatry (Mačiulaitis et al., 2008; Popik, Layer, and Skolnick, 1995; Belgers et al., 2016; Fernandez, 1982). It is no longer controversial among researchers to admit that the drugs currently employed by Western psychiatry are either ineffective or harmful (the side-effects outweighing the perceived benefits) and that categories of "mental illness" employed by Western psychiatry are culture-bound social constructs which do not have a biological basis:

"It is widely acknowledged that current psychiatric diagnostic schema and the treatments for psychiatric disorders lack a firm biological foundation...Categorizing patients by symptom checklists results in enormous clinical heterogeneity within diagnostic categories, surprisingly poor interrater reliability for many common psychiatric diagnoses (Freedman et al., 2013), *and very likely, poorer clinical outcomes.*" (Wang and Krystal, 2014, pp. 638-639; emphasis my own)

Scholars such as the psychologists Thomas Szasz, R.D. Laing, Félix Guattari, the historian of ideas Michel Foucault, and the philosopher Gilles Deleuze have been making the point for decades that "mental illness" is socially constructed, and they have likewise been making the point for decades that Western psychiatry yields poor clinical outcomes. Psychiatry has not progressed much further than Ken Kesey's descriptions in his novel *One Flew Over the Cuckoo's Nest* (1963). Only now, lobotomies and electro-shock therapy have been replaced by chemical lobotomies and chemical equivalents of electro-shock therapy (e.g. anti-psychotics and tranquilizers). One form of domination has replaced another.

In the broader scheme of psychiatry, the shift from psychoanalysis to pharmaceutical psychiatry is exemplary of what Deleuze (1990/1992) describes as the replacement of *disciplinary societies* with *societies of control*: "*Control* is the name [William S.] Burroughs proposes as a term for the new monster, one that Foucault recognizes as our immediate future. Paul Virilio also is continually analyzing the ultrarapid forms of free-floating control that replaced the old disciplines operating in the time frame of a closed system" (Deleuze, 1990/1992, p. 4). The faith in the psychiatrist as a holy shaman is being replaced, has been replaced, by faith in medicine as the food of the gods—the psychiatrist who reads from the checklist is a shaman devoid of glamour, a bureaucrat in the service of of the holy corporation (which, like Nicholas of Cusa's God, is a circle without circumference whose center is everywhere), who will give us the magic words which will allow us to acquire whenever we desire the food of the gods which will cure our ailment, however temporarily; it is no longer necessary to attend regular sessions with an analyst, we may acquire our ambrosia whenever we need it from free-floating pharmacies, instant gratification.

Thus, the scope of the present work is limited, for it focuses on psychoanalysis, an artifact of a disciplinary society, and neuropsychoanalysis, an archaism of a disciplinary society desperately attempting to adapt to the new society of control in which we are immersed. The present work, for the most part, does not deal with the much more ominous and imminent threat to human freedom, the society of control, and the molecular and chemical means (viz. pharmaceuticals) through which it controls human beings.

The Oedipus complex, like the majority of Freud's concepts, is a social construct, not a scientific truth. Foucault and Deleuze and Guattari have already gone at length to criticize Oedipus and psychoanalysis. Citing Foucault (1961/2006), Deleuze and Guattari (1972/1977) comment upon the moralistic and ideological nature of Oedipus:

"Insofar as psychoanalysis cloaks insanity in the mantle of a "parental complex," and regards the patterns of self-punishment resulting from Oedipus as a confession of guilt, its theories are not at all radical or innovative. On the contrary: *it is completing the task begun by nineteenth-century psychology*, namely, to develop a moralized, familial discourse of mental pathology, linking madness to the "half-real, half-imaginary dialectic of the Family," deciphering within it "the unending attempt to murder the father," "the dull thud of instincts hammering at the solidity of the family as an institution and at its most archaic symbols". Hence, instead of participating in an undertaking that will bring about genuine liberation, psychoanalysis is taking part in the work of bourgeois [socio-political] repression at its most far-reaching level, that is to say, keeping European humanity harnessed to the yoke of daddy-mummy and *making no effort to do away with this problem once and for all.*" (Deleuze and Guattari, 1972/1977, p. 50)

Solms and the Neuropsychoanalysis Association (NPSA), by producing apologetics of Freud, are dragging nineteenth century psychology into the twenty first century. Not only are Freud's concepts factually wrong, but they are also socially conservative. Oedipus, the reservoir from which all psychoanalytic discourse flows and to which it all returns, is a social construct which is used to propagate bourgeois ideology and preserve the bourgeois institution of family. Furthermore, psychoanalysis hinders a scientific understanding of the mind. Although neuroscience comprehensively disproves Freud, from specific claims to foundational concepts, Solms and the NPSA fraudulently maintain that neuroscience legitimates psychoanalysis: by doing so, they too hinder scientific progress.

As it regards the empirical necessity of our work being a work in progress, we may détournement Freud:

"This in turn raises a host of other questions to which we can at present find no answer. We must be patient and await fresh methods and occasions of research. We must be ready, too, to abandon a path that we have followed for a time, if it seems to be leading to no good end. Only believers, who demand that science shall be a substitute for the catechism they have given up, will blame an investigator for developing or even transforming his views. We may take comfort, too, for the slow advances of our scientific knowledge in the words of the poet [al-Hariri]: ['What we cannot reach flying we must reach limping...The Book tells us it is no sin to limp.']" (Freud, 1920/1961, pp. 58-59)

We hope to raise more questions than provide answers. Let us proceed, then, to draw a map of the human mind, and like Félix Guattari, to raise the cry of the work in progress:

"As in painting or literature, the concrete performance of these cartographies requires that they evolve and innovate, that they open up new futures, without their authors (*auteurs*) having prior recourse to assured theoretical principles or to the authority of a group, a school or an academy...Work in progress!" (Guattari, 1989/2000, p. 40)

The Unity of Mind and Body

In everyday life, *mind* is usually used to refer to a subject which experiences, and *brain* is usually used to refer to a physical organ. The brain is viewed as being a part of the body, and the mind is viewed as something mysterious which is not quite capable of being understood. This view is folk psychology, and it does not accord with the facts.

The Cartesian relationship of mind to body is able to be formulated as a problem because of implicit assumptions and faulty reasoning. The mind-body problem is unempirical. To be more specific, the concept of *mind* which is employed in formulations of the mind-body problem is unempirical.

Descartes (1637/1968) claimed that the mind and body are different substances, and that the substance that is the mind exists independently of the body (p. 54). *Mind* for Descartes (1637/1968) is something akin to the concept of *soul* in religion and mysticism, an imperishable entity which remains alive even when the body dies (p. 54). Descartes's reasoning reveals much about the basic assumptions of the mind-body problem.

Descartes (1637/1968) begins his fourth discourse, in which he proposes what is now known as Cartesian dualism, by claiming he is searching for truth; his purported method of finding the truth is to doubt everything "in order to see if there did not remain after that anything in my belief which was entirely indubitable" (p. 53). Descartes's (1637/1968) doubt extends to the senses: "So, because our senses sometimes play us false, I decided to suppose that there was nothing at all which was such as they cause us to imagine it" (p. 53).

The "method" of Descartes is radically different than the scientific method.

Scientists also recognize that the senses sometimes play us false, but that does not provide scientists with sufficient evidence to disregard altogether the evidence which the senses provide, or which the instruments of the senses provide. To overcome the barrier of one individual's faulty senses, science relies on instruments of measurement and reproducibility. By being able to measure a given phenomenon, a record of it exists independent of an individual observer. By reproducing results, having many observers measure the same phenomenon, a consensus as to the accuracy of the measure may be reached.

Descartes, however, thought there was no knowledge whatsoever that the senses could provide about the mind. He rejects the scientific method and relies solely on his own subjective judgement of truth and falsehood. His subjective judgement leads him to his famous statement, "I think therefore I am", which he considers to be an indubitable truth (Descartes, 1637/1968, pp. 53-54). The phrase "I think therefore I am" is often rendered as *cogito ergo sum*; *cogito* being Descartes's concept of *mind*.

What is the mind for Descartes? He describes the mind in the following way:

"I thereby concluded that I was a substance, of which the whole essence or nature consists in thinking, and which, in order to exist, needs no place and depends on no material thing; so that this 'I', that is to say, the mind, by which I am what I am, is entirely distinct from the body, and even that it is easier to know than the body, and moreover, that even if the body were not, it would not cease to be all that it is." (Descartes, 1637/1968, p. 54)

By rejecting the possibility of evidence from the sensory world—that is, the material world—Descartes is free to do away with causality, and thus free to posit *mind* as an entity which is not bound by causality and therefore immortal. Furthermore, the mind is posited as being a different substance than the body—in other words, whereas the body is material, the mind is immaterial.

What evidence does Descartes provide for his conclusions? The evidence of his imagination; in the section directly preceding the above quoted passage, Descartes (1637/1968) writes:

"Then, examining attentively what I was, and seeing that I could pretend that I had no body and that there was no world or place that I was in, but that I could not, for all that, pretend that I did not exist, and that, on the contrary, from the very fact that I thought of doubting the truth of other things, it followed very evidently and very certainly that I existed; while on the other hand, if I had only ceased to think, although all the rest of what I had ever imagined had been true, I would have had no reason to believe that I existed." (p. 54)

Descartes argues that just because he is able to doubt the existence of the world outside of him and imagine that the world outside of him does not exist, the world outside of him does not necessarily exist. Descartes, having given up evidence drawn from the senses, and thus having renounced scientific experiments in the quest for knowledge, relies instead on a highly subjective thought experiment. Someone other than Descartes may very well be capable of imagining that their self does not exist, and another might be incapable of imagining that they have no body or that they exist without occupying a place in space and time. Descartes's thought experiment is not well-founded.

Moreover, it is impossible to reason that the world outside of one's self does not exist solely because one's self is capable of doubting its existence. This particular flaw in reasoning is known as an Appeal to Ignorance: arguing that a given phenomenon does not exist (or does exist) due to uncertainty about its existence. Just because the senses sometimes play us false does not necessarily mean that they always play us false, and just because one is able to doubt the existence of the world of the senses does not necessarily mean that the world of the senses does not exist.

There is no sufficient evidence to doubt the existence of a world independent of the mind, a material world. Since all the evidence points to the existence of a material world, it is more outlandish to claim that the material world does not exist, therefore the burden of proof falls on those who claim the non-existence of the material world.

Furthermore, Descartes confuses *thought* and *being*. Descartes (1637/1968) writes that his self is "a substance, of which the whole essence or nature consists in thinking" (p. 53). Descartes's concept of thought, however, is an auxiliary capability of being. The self, at the fundamental or "core" level, does not arise from thinking as Descartes understands thinking, which may be characterized roughly as "rational thought". Selfhood (consciousness) is experienced, at its "core", as a visceral feeling, an emotion (Damasio, 1999; Damasio, 2010; Solms, 2013; Panksepp, 1998). The "core" of being—more specifically, the being of a conscious organism—is affect.

To the reader acquainted with modern neuroscience, it may seem like a triviality to state that the mind is an organ of the body. However, cognitive science still suffers from the Descartes's errors of reasoning. The theory of *embodied cognition*, that the operations of the mind are limited and even determined by the organism's morphology and environment, still faces opposition from traditional cognitive scientists who diminish or ignore the role of the body in cognition (Shapiro, 2007). One of the leading figures of traditional cognitive science, Noam Chomsky, has even gone so far as to praise Cartesian dualism:

"The Cartesians tried to show that when the theory of corporeal body is sharpened and clarified and extended to its limits, it is still incapable of accounting for facts that are obvious to introspection and that are also confirmed by our observation of the actions of other humans. In particular, it cannot account for the normal use of human language, just as it cannot explain the basic properties of thought. Consequently, it becomes necessary to invoke an entirely new principle – in Cartesian terms, to postulate a second substance whose essence is thought, alongside of body, with its essential properties of extension and motion...I will return to this argument and the ways in which it was developed. But I think it is important to stress that, with all its gaps and deficiencies, it is an argument that must be taken seriously. There is nothing at all absurd in the conclusion."
(Chomsky, 2006, pp. 5-6)

The above quoted passage, first published in 1968 and reprinted in 2006, is not only theoretically unsound, but also factually outdated. The theory of embodied cognition applied to linguistics has made significant contributions to the understanding of language processing (Jirak et al., 2010), as has neurobiology, especially in recent decades. But Wernicke and Broca were already demonstrating how the mind is produced by the brain in the 19th century with their studies on the physiology of aphasia, and neurosurgeons in Peru and Egypt thousands of years ago were likewise demonstrating how the mind is produced by the brain, if only in practice and not in theory. Humanity has been slow in catching up with itself. Although Shapiro (2007) writes of embodied cognition and computational cognitive science as opposed to each other, Symons and Calvo (2014) demonstrate that the information processing of the organism depends on the body as well, hence the title of their essay "Computing with Bodies". In fact, there is a growing demand, corresponding to a growing need, for biologically based computational models of the mind (Wang and Krystal, 2014). Contrary to Chomsky's claim, Cartesian dualism (and dualism at large) is indeed absurd in its conclusion, precisely because of all its gaps and deficiencies. (Although we offer this critique of a passage by Chomsky, we acknowledge that the present work is indebted to his linguistic and political works).

The mind-body problems is not really a problem if the question of what is mind is approached from an empirical, materialist perspective. The mind-body problem has persisted into the twenty first century, viz. under the guise of Chalmer's "hard problem", because materialist theories of mind would mean having to accept that people are *mortal* and that there is no immortal soul—i.e., one of the only remaining superstitions of religion will have to be debunked, just as its other superstitions (e.g., creationism, geocentrism) have already been debunked. Empirically, the mind *is* the brain, and the brain *is* the mind. We note that the idea of consciousness being an emergent property of the brain is consistent with materialist reductionism, insofar as consciousness, when conceived of as emergent, is still made of matter. Furthermore, along the lines of emergentism, it can be concluded that concepts, philosophy, society, and culture are emergent phenomena of the brain, and thus that they too are material (e.g. concepts are material entities within the brain, an aggregate of electrochemical impulses). Thus, anthropology and sociology are materialist sciences which ultimately refer to material processes in the brain, but which of necessity due to the complexity of their subject matter, describe the discursive and the conceptual, i.e., the emergent phenomena. The theory of embodied cognition simply goes a bit further than stating that mind and brain are one—*the mind is the body, and the body is the mind.*

Consciousness Is A Biological Phenomenon

David Chalmers (2010) claims that there are two different types of problems of consciousness: the easy problems, and the hard problem. The easy problems, Chalmers (2010) writes, are those which can be answered by science, specifically cognitive science and neuroscience, and the hard problem cannot be solved by cognitive science or neuroscience (p. 4). Like Descartes, Chalmers assumes a-priori that there is a special quality of the mind (for Chalmers, a specific aspect of the mind, consciousness), which cannot be explained by the evidence of the senses (in Chalmers's case, cognitive science and neuroscience). Just as with the mind-body problem, the hard problem arises due to a confusion over words and definitions and a-priori assumptions.

Chalmers (2010) defines the hard problem in the following way:

"The really hard problem of consciousness is the problem of experience. When we think and perceive, there is a whir of information processing, but there is also a subjective aspect. As Nagel (1974) has put it, there is *something it is like* to be a conscious organism. This is subjective aspect is experience." (p. 5)

Chalmers's assumptions are clear: a) experience eludes scientific explanation, and b) experience is distinct and separate from information processing. Chalmers writes that Nagel once wrote that "there is *something it is like* to be a conscious organism". As mentioned earlier, the evidence from neuroscience suggests that consciousness is affect; at any given moment, a conscious organism has a particular affect, and that emotion is what it is like to be that conscious organism at that given time. Subjectivity means our feelings. The experience of consciousness is the experience of emotions. To use Damasio's (1999) phrase, consciousness is "the feeling of what happens".

Emotions—and thus experience, consciousness, and subjectivity—are capable of being explained by neuroscience.

Chalmers's distinctions, then, are unfounded. There is no "hard problem of consciousness", and all mental phenomena can indeed be reduced to material processes and be described in terms of information processing and neurophysiology.

Chalmers (2010) asks "Why should physical processing give rise to a rich inner life at all? It seems objectively unreasonable that it should, and yet it does" (p. 5). There is nothing "objectively unreasonable" that physical processing can give rise to a rich inner life; in fact, the *objective* point of view would be that of materialist reductionism. Due to his rejection of scientific evidence, it is reasonable to infer that Chalmers is not objective, and thus that his appeal to objectivity is anything but objective. He says the materialist reductionist position is "objectively unreasonable", which seems to mean nothing more than that it offends his sensibilities.

Chalmers (2010) states his distinction of easy problems and the hard problem in another way:

"The easy problems are easy precisely because they concern the explanation of cognitive abilities and functions. To explain a cognitive function, we need only specify a mechanism that can perform the function. The methods of cognitive science are well suited for this sort of explanation and so are well suited to the easy problems of consciousness. By contrast, the hard problem is hard precisely because it is not a problem about the performance of functions. The problem persists even when the performance of all of the relevant functions is explained." (p. 6)

Once again, Chalmers asserts that there is an inexplicable difference between consciousness and other cognitive functions. This distinction, however, remains an unproveable assertion, like Chalmers's other distinctions. Consciousness is precisely a cognitive function, and thus it can be adequately explained by specifying a mechanism that can perform the function. There is no sufficient evidence to suggest that consciousness is not a cognitive function; consciousness is altered by altering brain chemistry, and it ceases when brain activity ceases, these and a plethora of myriad phenomena observed by neuroscientists make it reasonable to infer that consciousness is generated by the brain. The burden of proof lies upon the metaphysicians to furnish the evidence that consciousness cannot be explained by biology because it is the more speculative claim and no such evidence currently exists. Perhaps the identity of consciousness as a cognitive function is easier to comprehend if we remember that consciousness is affect. Affects are indeed cognitive functions.

Konieczny, Roterman-Konieczna, and Spólnik (2014) write in their textbook on systems biology that "In biology, structure dictates function" (p. 1). It is a basic principle of biology that structure determines function, from molecular biology to anatomy. This theoretical point is supported by a large body of evidence and can be used to predict the behavior of biological systems. Thus, it is wholly supported by the basic principles of biology to infer that consciousness, a phenomenon occurring in biological organisms and therefore a biological phenomenon, is produced by a structure in the brain.

Konieczny et al. (2014) go on to write:

"In biology, structure and function are tightly interwoven. This phenomenon is closely associated with the principles of evolution. Evolutionary development has produced structures which enable organisms to develop and maintain its architecture, perform actions and store the resources needed to survive." (p. 1)

In the above quoted passage, we find an answer to Chalmers's question "Why should physical processing give rise to a rich inner life at all?" The answer is simple: natural selection. Organisms possessing consciousness have a significant advantage over organisms without consciousness. Consciousness is produced by a structure of the brain, and if the evolution of this structure is understood, then the evolution of consciousness, the reason why physical processing gives rise to a rich inner life, is understood as well.

Chalmers (2010) defines consciousness thusly: "In this central sense of "consciousness," an organism is conscious if there is something it is like to be that organism, and a mental state is conscious if there is something it is like to be in that state" (p. 5). We identify the vague phrase "something it is like to be" as a specific mental phenomenon, emotion. A conscious organism has an emotion—it feels like something to be that organism. So, to be more specific regarding consciousness and evolution: emotions and the neurological structures which produce emotions evolved by natural selection because they provided an evolutionary advantage to the organisms which possessed them.

Chalmers (2010), however, takes an extra precaution to make sure that one does not arrive at scientific explanations of consciousness: he arbitrarily makes a trivial distinction between *consciousness* "for the phenomena of experience" and *awareness* "for the more straightforward phenomena" (pp. 5-6). We have already proven how consciousness, if defined solely as experience, can be explained by material causes. However, let us examine Chalmers's distinction more closely.

The "straightforward phenomena" which Chalmers (2010) refers to, and which he would like to exclude from the definition of consciousness, are the phenomena which he identifies as belonging to the territory of "easy problems", in other words, cognitive functions:

"• the ability to discriminate, categorize, and react to environmental stimuli
• the integration of information by a cognitive system
• the reportability of mental states
• the ability of a system to access its own internal states
• the focus of attention
• the deliberate control of behavior
• the difference between wakefulness and sleep"
(p. 4)

By excluding the above listed phenomena from a definition of consciousness, Chalmers creates the illusion that consciousness is

incapable of being explained by science. However, even if we limit
our definition of consciousness to experience, as Chalmers does,
there is no sufficient reason why we would need to exclude the
above listed phenomena from our definition of experience.
Experience, and consciousness, can be described aptly as "the ability
to discriminate, categorize, and react to environmental stimuli", "the
integration of information by a cognitive system", and "the ability of
a system to access its own internal states".

Consciousness is synonymous with awareness, both
semantically and if we critically examine Chalmers's specialized and
arbitrary distinction. An experience is always an experience *of
something*—an *environment*, whether external or internal (the
body)—and "the ability of a system to access its own internal states"
is an apt description of an "inner life".

Chalmers's errors are comparable to those of Descartes's:
both reject the scientific method, both assume a-priori that
mind/consciousness is inherently different from material
phenomena, and both quibble over words and write fanciful rhetoric.
For similar reasons, there is neither a mind-body problem, nor is
there a hard problem of consciousness.

Although in this section we have compared the mind-body
problem of Descartes with the hard problem of Chalmers, we must
clarify what we mean by mind, and consciousness. *Mind* and
consciousness are not synonymous. Consciousness is only a part of
the mind—the mind also has unconscious processes. Consciousness
is the feeling, or sensation, of being. *Mind* includes both
consciousness and unconscious cognitive functions. Because of the
intimate relation of the brain and the body—especially the brain
stem structures which produce consciousness—*being* is not wholly
distinct from *mind* and *consciousness*.

Although both the unconscious and consciousness of the
mind can be defined by "the ability to discriminate, categorize, and
react to environmental stimuli" and "the integration of information
by a cognitive system", the system consciousness is distinguished by
its ability "to access its own internal states". Experience, as it is
defined by Chalmers, is synonymous with consciousness. However,
we object on empirical grounds to equating consciousness with
experience. Unconscious experiences are well documented,
especially in the case of split-brain patients (Solms and Turnbull,

2002, 82-83; Galin, 1974, p. 573). We define experience as "the ability to discriminate, categorize, and react to environmental stimuli", and consistent with our definition of the unconscious mind, we posit that unconscious experiences occur. Consciousness, which the neuroscientists Damasio (1999; 2010), Panksepp (1998), and Solms (2013) identify as affect, is a particular kind of experience—the access of internal states. Taking the hard problem seriously has been a serious hinderance to psychology and philosophy in the late twentieth and early twenty first century. The hard problem, as a social construct, gives credence to the metaphysics of bourgeois ideologies, including psychoanalysis and neuropsychoanalysis.

Damasio (1999; 2010) locates "core consciousness", the baseline of or bare minimum of consciousness, in a part of the upper brainstem called the periaqueductal gray, or PAG for short; The PAG is responsible for the production of emotional states—our baseline of consciousness is emotion. Damasio (1999; 2010) conceptualizes other functions of consciousness (such as memory, language, abstract reasoning, etc.), which require the cortex, as "extended consciousness". If core consciousness is obliterated, extended consciousness is obliterated as well, but damage to extended consciousness leaves core consciousness intact, though possibly impaired (Damasio, 1999; 2010). Some even live without a cortex—without extended consciousness—for example, hydranencephalic patients, who are born without a cortex (Merker, 2007; Solms, 2013). The cortex, even if it may be active, is in itself unconscious—it requires core consciousness to activate it in order for the information it harbors to become conscious (Solms, 2013). Although certain cortical areas also have specific functions (for example, relating to aspects of memory, language, abstract reasoning, etc.), most of the cerebral cortex is called the "association cortex" because it stores associations which have been learned via associative learning; its function is analogous to random-access-memory, or RAM, in a PC; and information in the cortex tends towards becoming automatized (towards *automaticity*), i.e., towards becoming automatically and unconsciously (implicitly) active, without the need for becoming conscious (Solms, 2013, pp. 12-14).

Metapsychology, Part I: The Metapsychology of Mark Solms and Oliver Turnbull

There is no straightforward definition of "metapsychology". Freud invented the concept *metapsychology*. Many scholars recognize that Freud's use of the concept metapsychology is often inconsistent and vague, and when it is discernible, based on outdated concepts like Lamarckian inheritance and physicalism (Holt, 2002, pp. 337-341). We shall return later to Freud's concept of metapsychology. First, we shall examine critically the psychoanalysts Mark Solms's and Oliver Turnbull's concept of metapsychology, which is clearly defined and relates to Chalmers's hard problem.

To understand Solms's and Turnbull's concept of metapsychology, we must examine their answer to Chalmers's hard problem. Solms's and Turnbull's (2002) response to the hard problem is a position which they call "dual-aspect monism": "*Dual-aspect monism* accepts that we are made of only one type of stuff (that is why it is a *monist* position), but it also suggests that this stuff is *perceived* in two different ways (hence, *dual-aspect* monism)" (p. 56).

At first glance, Solms's and Turnbull's position appears to be the materialist one, that mind and brain are both made of matter but are perceived in two different ways (subjectively as the mind, objectively as the brain); this however, is not what Solms and Turnbull mean by dual-aspect monism. Solms and Turnbull (2002) go on to elaborate their position: "The important point to grasp about this otherwise straightforward position is that it implies that *in our essence* we are *neither* mental nor physical beings—at least not in the sense that we normally employ these terms" (p. 56).

The phrase "dual-aspect monism", then, is a misnomer. To the either/or question of "are we mind or brain?", the monist answer would "both mind and brain, for mind and brain are one". Solms's and Turnbull's (2002) dual-aspect monism, however, answers that we are "neither mind nor brain", and posits a third substance which generates both mind and brain (pp. 56-58). "Dual-aspect monism", then, is more trialism than monism. There are, however, much more grievous problems with dual-aspect monism; they can be summarized by the objection that to not be a physical being means to be a metaphysical being.

The beginning of Solms's and Turnbull's (2002) proof is promising:

"When I perceive myself externally (in the mirror, for example) and internally (through introspection), I am perceiving the *same thing* in two different ways (as *body* and *mind*, respectively). This distinction between body and mind is therefore *an artifact of perception*. My external perceptual apparatus sees me (my body) as a physical entity, and my internal perceptual apparatus feels me (my self) as a mental entity. These two things are one and the same thing— there *really* is only one "me"—but since I am the very thing that I am observing, I perceive myself from two different viewpoints simultaneously." (p. 56)

Without any other context, the above passage would serve as a convincing argument in favor of materialist reductionism (or materialist monism), and it would indeed make the case of dualism harder to defend. But Solms's and Turnbull's intention is otherwise; Solms and Turnbull (2002), in fact, are opposed to materialist reductionism (p. 52). As soon as Solms and Turnbull (2002) seemingly refute the mind-body dichotomy, they reinstate it:

"We can never literally *perceive* the stuff we are made of without first representing it through one of our perceptual modalities—which means that we can never escape the artificial mind-body dichotomy. Since we can never transcend the limits of our senses, we can never perceive the *underlying* mind-body stuff *directly*." (pp. 56-57)

Although Solms and Turnbull profess to be monists, the argument they employ in the above quoted passage is reminiscent of dualism; it is at this point metaphysics and not science. Solms's and Turnbull's argument, by emphasizing the fundamental difference between "mind-body stuff" (which, in their thought, cannot be directly perceived) and "mind/body" (which can be directly perceived), resembles Cartesian dualism. More accurately, however, Solms's and Turnbull's position is not dualism, but trialism: there are three substances, mind, body, and mind-body stuff. In Solms's and

Turnbull's (2002) thought, the difference between "mind-body stuff" and "mind/body" is irreconcilable: "we can *never* perceive the underlying mind-body stuff directly" [Italics my own] (p. 57).

The purported problem of perceptual viewpoint of mind, body, and mind-body stuff on which Solms's argument rests is not evidence based. The mind-body dichotomy as an artifact of perception is a particular kind of artifact of perception—an illusion. Damasio (2010) compares the illusion which gives rise to the mind-body dichotomy to the illusion of the sun circling the earth which gave rise to geocentric models of the universe:

"Our intuition tells us that the mercurial, fleeting business of the mind lacks physical extension. I believe this intuition is false and attributable to the limitations of the unaided self. I see no reason to give to it any more credence than to previously evident and powerful intuitions such as the pre-Copernican view of what the sun does to the earth or, for that matter, the view that the mind resides in the heart. Things are not always what they seem. White light is a composite of the colors of the rainbow, although that is not apparent to the naked eye." (p. 15)

It is the scientific method to test claims, as opposed to the commonsense notion of trusting one's intuition. The everyday observations of the sun's relation to the earth is that the sun circles the earth—the sun "goes up" and "goes down". However, with special instruments, most notably the telescope, new evidence is furnished which reveals the actual relation—the earth circles the sun. In an analogous illusion, equipped only with "the naked eye", one observes that one can see one's own body, but one cannot see one's own mind. The solution, too, is analogous to the use of a telescope to observe "the heavens"—with the use of special instruments such as fMRI, one can indeed observe the mind in action. Let us refer to the inability of the naked eye to observe the self as "the illusion of the invisible self".

The illusion of the invisible self is a perceptual illusion, an "artifact of perception", comparable to the geocentric illusion, or even to optical illusions. A large part of the problem is in the definition of *perception*.

What is considered to be perception is culturally relative. Whereas in Western civilization, the senses are traditionally divided into five (sight, sound, smell, taste, and touch), other cultures have different categories of perception. For example, the Hausa recognize only two senses, and the Javanese have five senses which do not all coincide with the Western five (the senses recognized by the Javanese are sight, sound, smell, feeling, and talking) (Howes, 1991; Dundes, 1980, p. 92).

Moreover, apart from sight, the emphasis of other senses in our experience of the world varies across cultures (San Roque et al., 2015). San Roque et al. (2015) found that "sight is a dominant sense" (p. 31), which "provides strong support for the vision dominance hypothesis, suggesting a "common core" of human experience in perceptual language" (p. 49). Cultural variability affects an individual's ability to use a given sense. A study by Majid and Burenhult (2014) found that English speakers, who lack words for smells, are worse at identifying smells than the Jahai of the Malay Penninsula, who have more words for smells. Moreover, the scientific study of the senses includes as senses nociception (the sense of pain) and thermoception (the sense of temperature), among many others.

A combination of the dominance of vision in the human sensorium and the overreliance of vision at the expense of other senses in the West, in addition to the limitations imposed by the conceptual framework of the traditional division of the senses into five in Western culture, may help explain why the illusion of the invisible self has persisted into the 21st century, a time of incredible scientific and technological advances. From the first-person perspective, one's own consciousness cannot be seen, heard, smelled, touched, or tasted. Thus, it appears as if the self is invisible and irreducible to material processes.

However, if we move beyond ethnocentric attitudes and beliefs about the human sensorium, and we instead embrace the neuroscience of perception, then it becomes evident that one does indeed perceive the mind.

Even Solms, who is a neuroscientist as well as a psychoanalyst, cannot help but refer to subjective awareness as something that is perceived, which causes an internal contradiction in the position of "dual-aspect monism", since the individual is able to perceive the mind which belongs to it, but is incapable of perceiving "the underlying mind-body stuff":

"Since we can never transcend the limits of our senses, we can never perceive the *underlying* mind-body stuff *directly*. We can only make *inferences* from the data of perception (from scientific observation) as to the nature of that underlying entity—let's call it the *"human mental apparatus"*—and inferences about how it is constructed and how it works. Our picture of the mental apparatus *itself* will therefore always be a figurative one—a model. We possess concrete perceptual images of its two observable manifestations (the brain and subjective awareness), but the underlying entity that *lies behind* those perceptual images will never be directly observable. Scientific observation has its limits." (Solms and Turnbull, 2002, p. 57)

Panksepp et. al (2012) include among the most phylogenetically ancient emotions, or as they say, "primary-process, basic-primordial affective states", "homeostatic affects" and "sensory affects", "sensory affects" being defined as "exteroceptive-sensory triggered pleasurable and unpleasurable/disgusting feelings" (p. 7). Thermoception, the sense of temperature, may be classified as a homeostatic affect—we *feel* cold or we *feel* hot, and these feelings are experienced as conscious states. Nociception, the sense of pain, may be classified as a sensory affect—pain is often a feeling of unpleasure, and it is experienced as a conscious state. So, although from the first-person point of view consciousness is invisible, it is still perceived. The Javanese are well justified in considering feeling to be a mode of perception. Since consciousness can be perceived, we can infer that it is made of matter and energy, or mass-energy, like everything else which can be perceived.

The existence of a "human mental apparatus" which "lies behind" the mind and the brain is an unfounded assertion, like Bobby Henderson's Flying Spaghetti Monster. Non-materialist-reductionist theories of mind can all be described as "The Flying Spaghetti Monster Theory of Mind" because they all posit the mind to be a metaphysical entity. Since affects—which are synonymous with consciousness—can be explained as products of the activities of groups of neurons, there is no necessity to posit an immaterial entity such as the "human mental apparatus" in order to explain the mind.

Solms and Turnbull claim that "scientific observation has its limits"—in the context of his explication of dual-aspect monism, such a claim is tantamount to admitting that the study of the "human mental apparatus", which is what he referred to earlier as "mind-body stuff", is not science but that it is nonetheless somehow valid.

What is the study of the "human mental apparatus"? Solms and Turnbull (2002) define it as *metapsychology*:

"Freud described this type of model building as "metapsychology". This term refers to our attempts to see beyond [*meta*] consciousness [*psyche*]. Freud contrasted metapsychology with *metaphysics*, which is a branch of philosophy concerned with similar problems, but which attempts to solve them through pure reason rather than scientific observation and experimentation." (p. 57)

Solms and Turnbull paradoxically claim that there exists a "human mental apparatus" which cannot be scientifically observed, and that metapsychology (the study of the "human mental apparatus") is a science which relies on scientific observation and experimentation. The two claims are irreconcilable. Either a "human mental apparatus" does not exist (which renders a metapsychology wholly unnecessary), or metapsychology is not a science (which means that a "human mental apparatus" does not exist). If metapsychology uses scientific observation and experimentation, then it excludes from its field of the study the "human mental apparatus", since a "human mental apparatus" cannot be scientifically observed; however, since the existence of a "human mental apparatus" is central to the definition of *metapsychology*, it seems that metapsychology invalidates itself. *Metapsychology is metaphysics.*

Solms and Turnbull (2002) claim validity for the "human mental apparatus" by comparing it to quarks and gravity:

"There are many things that scientists are concerned with that cannot be perceived directly. Witness, for example, the "quarks" of contemporary physics, or even the force of "gravity". Nobody doubts the existence of these ultimate things, yet they can only be observed via their perceived *effects*." (p. 57)

Comparing the hypothesis of a "human mental apparatus" to the study of quarks and gravity is a highly misleading equivocation.

Gravity-waves were and quarks are mathematical predictions. The "human mental apparatus" of Solms and Turnbull is not a mathematical prediction, it is metaphysical speculation.

Individual quarks are not visible due to physical constraints, not philosophical ones. Quarks possess a property referred to as *color*, although the term is somewhat misleading, as it does not refer to a frequency of light; the term *color* is merely an analogy. An individual quark can have one of three colors: red, green, or blue. An individual quark is never observed because quarks must pair in order to "make white light" (an analogy) and "hide" their "color". Quarks come in a triplet, called a baryon, which consists one red quark, one blue, and one green. Quarks also come in pairs, called mesons; a meson consists of a colored quark and an anti-colored quark, which "cancel out" and become "color neutral". The force which binds quarks to each other is called the "color force". The color force, unlike other observed forces, increases with distance instead of weakening. In addition, the energy required to separate quarks produces mesons long before they are far enough apart to be observed separately. (Rohlf, 1994, pp. 183-185)

Although they cannot be directly observed individually, quarks, and the rest of the Standard Model of quantum mechanics, is validated by decades of experiments. The Standard Model, which includes quarks, can be used to predict specific phenomena, and these specific phenomena can be observed in experiments. Thus, it is safe to infer the existence of quarks. Perhaps one day, the technology will be found to observe quarks individually, just as was the case with the Higgs boson, which was able to be observed due to the ATLAS and CMS experiments at CERN's Large Hadron Collider.

Solms and Turnbull published their book *The Brain and the Inner World*, in which they define metapsychology and dual-aspect monism, in 2002. There have been major advancements in the sciences in the fourteen years since they published their book. As it pertains to gravity, in 2016 a paper published by Abbott et al. revealed that gravity waves had been observed by the Laser Interferometer Gravitational-Wave Observatory, or LIGO; the observation took place on September 14, 2015. The gravity waves observed were produced by the merging of two black holes (Abbott et al., 2016, p. 1). The observation of gravity waves (which were mathematically predicted by Einstein in 1916), is the direct observation of gravity.

The "human mental apparatus", the "mind-body stuff" of Solms's and Turnbull's dual-aspect monism, is metaphysical. For Solms and Turnbull (2002), however, the "human mental apparatus" is more foundational than either mind or brain: "What can be inferred from these two (correlated) sets of data [brain processes and subjective processes] about the functional organization of the underlying apparatus that *generates* them?" [Italics my own] (p. 58). Solms and Turnbull actually consider the "human mental apparatus" as an entity which *generates* the processes of the mind and the body, in other words, they posit the "human mental apparatus" as an entity which *causes* the processes of the mind and the body. Such a postulate, if it were true, would elevate metapsychology (and by extension psychoanalysis), above every other branch of psychology. However, as we have demonstrated, the "human mental apparatus" does not exist, and metapsychology, as formulated by Solms and Turnbull, can never be anything more than pseudoscience.

Solms and Turnbull (2008) write that the hard problem is an illusion:

"If we accept that the mind-body problem thereby boils down to *a problem of observational viewpoint*, and that the distinction between your self and your body (between mind and matter) is therefore merely an artifact of perception, the "hard problem" evaporates." (p. 57)

However, Solms and Turnbull are gravely mistaken about the implications of the mind-body dichotomy being an illusion, and their position of dual-aspect monism, with which they attempt to answer the hard problem, is untenable. In any case, the hard problem is merely metaphysical quibbling to begin with. It is indeed the case that the mind-body problem is a "problem of observational viewpoint" and an "artifact of perception", but this is so only because the mind is reducible to matter and energy, or mass-energy. The hard problem "evaporates" for the same reason: the mind is reducible to the brain.

Metapsychology, Part II: The Metapsychology of Mark Solms and Oliver Turnbull Continued—More Philosophical Considerations

We have not yet exhausted all the arguments Solms and Turnbull (2002) present in favor of metapsychology—which, as we have already mentioned, is metaphysics and not science.

Solms and Turnbull (2002) write that some propositions, such as "God exists", are untestable, then go on to write that they "are of the opinion that the nature of the relationship between brain and mind (body and soul) is *not* amenable to scientific proof", just like the statement "God exists" (pp. 54-55). There are three major problems with this argument. The first is that empirically there is no mind-body problem, which we have already discussed; however, let us continue to examine their statements in greater detail.

The second is the equivocation of possible solutions to the mind-body problem with the proposition that God exists. This equivocation is strengthened by an almost inexplicable bait and switch: for the only time in the entire chapter "Mind and Brain—How Do They Relate?", *mind* is equated with *soul*. Solms and Turnbull (2002) spend the entire chapter (pp. 45-78) discussing Chalmer's hard problem and possible solutions to the hard problem, and this is the only place that mind and soul are equated—the bait and switch occurs with haste, in passing, in a single paragraph, and is never again mentioned: in addition to the above mention of soul, Solms and Turnbull (2002) write in the same paragraph, "Statements such as "body and soul are one" (the monist position) or "the soul does not really exist" (the materialist position) are not, in our view, scientifically testable concepts" (p. 55). The concepts *soul* and *mind* are not the same, hence why we have described the above passage as an equivocation. *Mind* and *consciousness* can be operationally defined and thus tested for. *Soul* cannot be tested for because it is a metaphysical entity, i.e., it is a social construct. It is intellectually dishonest to consistently discuss mind and consciousness only to all of a sudden reveal, without further explanation, that by *mind* they have meant *soul* all along. Furthermore, the proposition that "the soul does not exist" (if we mean the soul to be an immaterial entity, as it is traditionally defined) is true precisely because the soul cannot be observed or measured.

The third problem with Solms's and Turnbull's argument is that if all possible solutions to the mind-body problem are not amenable to scientific proof, then *their* solution to the mind-body problem—dual-aspect monism—*is also not amenable to scientific proof*. That is tantamount to admitting that dual-aspect monism and neuropsychoanalysis—which has dual-aspect monism as its philosophical basis—is tantamount to pseudo-science. As we have written in previous sections, dual-aspect monism and neuropsychoanalysis are indeed pseudoscientific, although the reason why is not because there is no scientific solution to the hard problem.

Furthermore, Solms and Turnbull (2002) ascribe to a false dichotomy between philosophy and science:

"It is possible to find some merit in all of these different philosophical positions. It is also possible with a little effort, to make all of them look ridiculous. This might be one good reason to replace the philosophical approach to the "hard" problem with a scientific one... Loath as we may be to admit it, the testable hypotheses that scientists can work with are embedded in sets of broader propositions that are themselves untestable...Science is limited to answering questions that can be asked *within* a particular world view; it cannot test the world view itself." (p. 54)

Philosophy and science are not mutually exclusive. Deleuze and Guattari (1991/1994) define philosophy as the discipline of studying and inventing concepts (pp. 1-12). Science is the empirical study of the world. Considering these definitions, there is necessarily a great deal of overlap between philosophy and science. An example of this overlap is cultural anthropology, which studies the beliefs and customs of different cultures—these beliefs and customs are dependent upon culturally relative social *concepts*. A more specific example from a different branch of science, physics: Einstein's concept of a unified spacetime was a *new concept* based upon empirical evidence and mathematical formulas that space and time are merely two different ways of describing the same phenomenon. (We go even further and claim that science is a branch of philosophy, since all science is natural philosophy, the study of the natural world).

Furthermore, worldviews *are* testable. For example, geocentrism and heliocentrism are both worldviews, and when tested for, it turns out that heliocentrism is true and that geocentrism is false. The neuroscience of the last few decades is for psychology what the Copernican revolution was for Western astronomy during the Renaissance.

Solms and Turnbull (2002), however, use their false dichotomy between philosophy and science in order to justify the conclusion that since all possible solutions to the hard problem are philosophical worldviews they are not amenable to scientific proof (pp. 54-55). However, the materialist position—that mind and consciousness are produced by mass-energy—is indeed amenable to scientific proof, and it is the only position which can be empirically proved. Thus, materialism is both a philosophical worldview and it is a scientific position. The immaterial can never be observed nor measured, thus dualism and idealism are not scientifically valid. And as we have already demonstrated, neither is dual-aspect monism. On the other hand, everything that can be observed and measured is a material entity, therefore one must conclude that mind and consciousness are made of mass-energy.

One may choose all kinds of theological or spiritual beliefs in one's personal life, but the scientific method is the application of the philosophical worldview of materialism (either explicitly or implicitly), no matter which culture it is employed in. Newton was a pious Christian, but his theory of gravity is a materialist theory, or at least strives to be a materialist theory. Material entities, entities made of mass-energy, can be empirically proven to exist; immaterial entities cannot be empirically proven to exist, and they can be inferred to be non-existent, i.e., imaginary, i.e., social constructs.

Solms and Turnbull (2002) criticize the materialist monist position—that everything is made of matter—for, among other things, speaking of the processes of the brain as *causing* mental processes (pp. 55-56). The organs and organ systems of our body are described by biology and medical science as being responsible for causing processes specific to them. For example, the digestive system causes digestion, the respiratory system causes breathing, etc. Claiming that the nervous system has a special and unique status which somehow exonerates it from the laws of biology—and by implication, the laws of physics and chemistry upon which biology depends—is nonsense. The brain is an organ of the body, and like any other organ, it has functions. One function of the brain is cognition—mental processes. In other words, a function of the brain is to generate, to *cause*, the mind and its mental processes.

Solms and Turnbull (2002) also conclude that all "mental science"—they explicitly include cognitive neuroscience and cognitive science in this category—is ultimately about metapsychology, "describing the functional architecture of the mental apparatus" (p. 291). Once again, they rely upon equivocation: they argue that the laws of nature described by science are all abstractions derived from nature, and that likewise the mind has as its scientifically inferred abstraction the mental apparatus (Solms and Turnbull, 2002, p. 292). This is a weak analogy. The laws of nature (the laws of physics, for example) are mathematical formalizations which can predict material events. Solms's and Turnbull's hypothesis of a mental apparatus cannot predict anything and is not mathematically formalized. The laws of nature can be empirically proven to exist; the mental apparatus cannot be empirically proven to exist.

The model-building of cognitive science is a fundamentally different activity than the model-building of metapsychology. The model-building of cognitive science is often mathematically formalized and can be empirically validated. For example, the connectome of a nervous system is a comprehensive map of its neural connections—it is one way of mapping the detailed structure of the nervous system. Connectomes are information-processing diagrams made by cognitive neuroscientists. Connectomes and other cognitive and neuroscientific diagrams differ radically in conception and purpose from the diagrams Freud presents in his essays. The two cannot be equated, as Solms and Turnbull (2002) attempt to do (p. 293).

To answer the question "Who needs psychoanalysis?", Solms and Turnbull (2002) write:

"The answer is that psychoanalysis gives us access to inner workings of the mental apparatus that cannot be studied—literally cannot be *seen*—from the "objective" point of view. Feelings are a perfect example. Feelings cannot be seen, but they most certainly *exist*." (p. 296)

However, feelings *can* be seen from an objective point of view: countless fMRI scans of emotional states prove it. The self-reports of a subject during neuroscience research have no necessity to be cloaked in psychoanalytic language. In fact, the implications of our deconstruction of neuropsychoanalysis suggests that it would damaging to neuroscience research to rely upon a psychoanalytical interpretation of self-reports rather than the self-reports themselves. Furthermore, Solms and Turnbull (2002) support the idea that animals other than humans have emotions (p. 113), following the neuroscience research of Panksepp (1998), which is performed from the "objective point of view" and lays a claim to being able to observe emotions with scientific instruments. This generates yet another contradiction—the objective viewpoint is being used to justify the existence of emotions in non-human animals in one section, and in another it is claimed that the objective viewpoint cannot observe emotions. To add to the absurdity, an entire chapter ("Emotion and Motivation", pp. 105-137) is devoted to using the neuroscience of emotion—the objective perspective on emotions—to attempt to legitimate psychoanalysis (Solms and Turnbull, 2014).

In conclusion, no one needs psychoanalysis. However, we feel that we will convince no one unless we give a more detailed account of our position.

Metapsychology, Part III: Introduction to the Metapsychology of Freud

The metapsychology of Freud consists of "psychological (or psychopathological) theorizing of the evolutionary biology of Lamarck and Haeckel, and the physicalistic physiology of his teachers and research supervisors in medical school" (Holt, 2002, p. 338). Freud's concept of metapsychology is the theoretical foundation of psychoanalysis, and metapsychology has as its foundations Lamarckian inheritance and physicalist physiology. More specifically, Freud's metapsychology consists of "dynamic, economic, and topographic *points of view*" (Holt, 2002, p. 338). The terms *dynamic, economic* and *topographic* are given special meanings by Freud:

"The dynamic point of view comprises conceptualizing motivational phenomena by the use of psychic forces. The economic point of view entails attempts to explain by quantitative variations in amounts of psychic energies. The topographic point of view means locating processes in the structural elements of the topographic model of Systems Cs., Pcs., and Ucs. [Consciousness, Preconscious, and Unconscious]." (Holt, 2002, p. 338)

The topographic model was revised by Freud throughout his career, but eventually came to mean "the structural model of ego, superego, and id" (Holt, 2002, p. 338). We shall examine all of these assumptions in turn.

Lamarckian Evolutionary Theory versus The Modern Synthesis

Lamarckian inheritance is the hypothesis that evolution is driven by the inheritance of acquired characteristics; for example, the classic giraffe example: from the Lamarckian point of view, giraffes evolved long necks because each generation, by stretching their necks, made the necks of their children longer. In contrast, the theory of natural selection posits that evolution is driven by the survival of the fittest. The evolution of giraffes from the point of view of natural selection: the ancestor of giraffes all had short necks, but a few developed long necks due to mutations, these long-necked giraffes performed better than the short-necked ones, thus the long-necked giraffes came to be dominant in the population and the short-necked giraffes went extinct.

Lamarckian inheritance, despite its intuitive appeal to folk psychology, is not supported by any evidence, and the theory of natural selection is supported by a large body of evidence. Phenomena such as genetic assimilation and transgenerational epigenetics have led some scientists to revive Lamarck (Skinner, 2015), even though accepting Lamarckian inheritance essentially means that one has misunderstood the Modern Synthesis (the synthesis of Darwin's theory of natural selection, Mendel's theory of genetics, and molecular biology). Genetic assimilation and transgenerational epigenetics are mechanisms which can only cause evolutionary changes *within* or *through* natural selection. Genetic assimilation and transgenerational epigenetics cannot cause speciation, the emergence of new species, by themselves.

The most decisive evidence against the Lamarckian hypothesis and in favor of natural selection comes from molecular biology, particularly from genetics. Ernst Mayr (2001) critiques Lamarckian inheritance as "soft inheritance":

"[Lamarckian] theory assumes that genetic material is "soft" and that it can be molded by environmental influences, and that these changes can then be transmitted to future generations by an "inheritance of acquired characteristics." This theory is based on a belief in soft inheritance." (p. 81)

In other words, the Lamarckian hypothesis depends on the notion that genes, the units of inheritance, can be altered by the use/disuse of a structure or by the direct influence of the environment. For instance, as Mayr (2001) writes, it was a commonly held assumption prior to Darwin that Africans had black skin because they had been darkened by the tropical sun for generations (p. 81). It is important to note that induced mutations, which are caused by DNA damage, are functionally different from acquired traits. The natural process of the sun darkening an individual's skin is not caused by changes to DNA, and such darkening of the skin is not passed on to an individual's offspring.

Summarizing decades of research on genetics, Mayr (2001) writes:

"…all experiments that tried to demonstrate [Lamarckism's] validity were unsuccessful. Mendelian genetics, by proving the constancy of genes, completely contradicted soft inheritance. Finally, it was shown by molecular biology that no information can be transmitted from the proteins of the body to the nucleic acids of the germ cells, in other words, that an inheritance of acquired characters does not take place. This is the so-called "central dogma" of molecular biology." (pp. 81-82)

At this point, two phenomena must be briefly discussed, for they are often erroneously taken to be proof that "Lamarck was right": transgenerational epigenetics and genetic assimilation. Epigenetics is the study of gene expression—genes can be turned on and off, affecting which traits are or are not expressed. Epigenetic changes do not mean changes in the DNA sequence of an organism—epigenetic changes leave the DNA itself unaltered. There is some evidence to support the concept of transgenerational epigenetics, patterns of gene *expression* which are passed on from parent to child, but most of this evidence comes from *plants*: "Although the inheritance of epigenetic characters can certainly occur—particularly in plants—how much is due to the environment and the extent to which it happens in humans remain unclear" (Heard and Martienssen, 2014, p. 95). An environmental stimulus can change the pattern of gene expression in a sexually reproducing organism, thus affecting which traits it expresses, and this epigenetic change *may* be passed on vertically to the organism's offspring. At first, this may bear a superficial resemblance to the "inheritance of acquired characteristics", since it appears as if an acquired trait is affecting subsequent generations. However, as was mentioned, epigenetic changes leave genes (the units of inheritance) *unaltered*, and it is through changes in DNA that speciation, or macroevolution, occurs. Furthermore, to what extent it is legitimate to describe an epigenetic change as an "acquired trait", especially as "acquired traits" are traditionally understood (for example, one's skin being darkened by the sun), is open to debate.

Epigenetic changes are normally "erased" or "reset" so that they are *not* vertically transmitted to offspring:

"Reprogramming is required to remove epigenetic signatures acquired during development or imposed by the environment so that subsequent elaboration of the body plan in the embryo properly reflects the genetic blueprint characteristic of each species. If germline reprogramming fails, epigenetic marks can be retained and could be transmitted from one generation to the next. As with classical (i.e., DNA sequence) mutations, most epigenetic "mutations" (epialleles) are either neutral or deleterious, frequently involving the unleashing of transposable elements and other genomic parasites. But transgenerational epigenetic inheritance also has the potential to be adaptive and, in some cases, might even respond to environmental challenges with major implications for heredity, breeding, and evolution." (Heard and Martienssen, 2014, p. 95)

Furthermore, although epigenetic inheritance is "relatively common in plants", it is rare in mammals (which includes humans):

"In mammals, efficient reprogramming occurs in the early embryo and in the germline. These two rounds of epigenetic erasure leave little chance for inheritance of epigenetic marks, whether programmed, accidental, or environmentally induced. Thus, although transmission of acquired states can occur in some animals (such as nematodes), proof that transgenerational inheritance has an epigenetic basis is generally lacking in mammals. *Indeed, evolution appears to have gone to great lengths to ensure the efficient undoing of any potentially deleterious bookmarking that a parent's lifetime experience may have imposed."* (Heard and Martienssen, 2014, p. 95; emphasis my own)

Whereas genes serve the function of transmitting traits down generations and thus are not "erased" or "reset" with each generation, epigenetic changes do not serve the function of transmitting traits down generations (which is why it is nature's program to erase them with each new generation). Transgenerational epigenetics is an anomaly and a rarity. Natural selection is the means by which traits are inherited and speciation occurs.

Scientists such as Springer (2015) who claim that transgenerational epigenetics provides support for a Lamarckian or a neo-Lamarckian theory of evolution are motivated by ideology, not empirical evidence. Lamarckian theory supports ideas of folk psychology, such as race (which is a social construct with no biological basis), and the idea that one inherits "the sins of the father". The concept of race maintains existing power structures and class hierarchies by a) subjugating a group of people arbitrarily deemed an "inferior race" and making them remain in the working class, and b) creating conflicts within the working class, "racial conflicts", which prevent the working class from uniting and fighting against their oppressors, the bourgeoisie. The idea of inheriting "the sins of the father" induces guilt and shame in the individual which keeps them in a submissive state, and it reduces all their real problems to imaginary family problems (it reduces all discourse to familial discourse, which is bourgeois ideology). Lamarckian theory is *implicitly* racist and ideological.

We refer the reader interested in learning more about transgenerational epigenetics to the essay "Transgenerational Epigenetic Inheritance: Myths and Mechanisms" by Edith Heard and Robert A. Martienssen (2014).

Hofer (2014), a proponent of neuropsychoanalysis, defends the Lamarckian foundation of Freud's psychoanalysis. Hofer (2014) presents, or rather misrepresents, an experiment by Skolnick et al. (1980), in which he was also a researcher, as evidence of the inheritance of acquired characteristics (Hofer, 2014, pp. 9-10).

Skolnick et al. (1980) demonstrated that:

"Premature separation of rat pups from their dams [mothers] greatly increases their susceptibility to restraint-induced gastric erosions [stress ulcers]. When prematurely separated female rats grow to adulthood and mate with stock males, their normally reared F_1 progeny also have increased susceptibility to restraint-induced erosions [stress ulcers]. Cross-fostering studies show that prenatal rather than postnatal factors transmit this susceptibility to F_1 progeny." (p. 1161)

To rephrase the above in slightly simpler language: when female rats highly susceptible to stress ulcers (due to their having been prematurely separated from their mothers) are bred with stock males, their normally raised offspring display increased susceptibility to stress ulcers (Skolnick et al., 1980; Hofer, 2014, pp. 9-10).

The normal time for rat pups to be separated from their mothers is 21 days after birth, and Skolnick et al. (1980) chose 14 days after birth as the date for premature separation (p. 1161). Skolnick et al. (1980) measured the frequency of stress ulcers in rats by attempting to induce stress ulcers via food deprivation and restraint, then murdering the rats and performing autopsies (p. 1161). Skolnick et al. (1980) found that 10-20% of the rats separated at the customary time developed stress ulcers, while 80-90% of the prematurely separated rat pups developed stress ulcers (p. 1161). But, of course, "the group of special interest was the normally separated progeny of mothers who had been prematurely separated in their own infancy", of which 64% developed stress ulcers—in contrast to the control group (normally separated progeny of normally separated mothers), of which about 19% developed stress ulcers (Skolnick et al., 1980, p. 1162). 80% of prematurely separated progeny of prematurely separated dams developed stress ulcers regardless of whether their foster mother was normally or prematurely separated (Skolnick et al., 1980, p. 1162).

The fact that the early development of the dams biologically affected their offspring is not in question; what is in question is the mechanism of vertical inheritance. There are reasons to suppose that the vertical inheritance reported by Skolnick et al. (1980) is not transgenerational epigenetics. Hofer (2014) himself presents these reasons, although he does so in a different context (the context of proving Freud right). Hofer and his colleagues, who have studied attachment and development in rat pups, include physical contact among a list of "hidden maternal regulators":

"We found that the behavioral and physiological systems of the infant were each regulated (that is, maintained at a certain level or in a certain pattern or rhythm) by different components of the mother-infant interaction prior to separation: by the mother's licking, warmth, odors, suckling, milk, and by the timing or rhythm with which these interactions occurred...We called them "hidden maternal regulators" because they were not apparent when simply observing the mother interacting with her offspring." (Hofer, 2014, p. 7)

Physical contact in the mother-child relationship helps maintain homeostasis and promote development in the infant (Hofer, 2014, p.7). This has been demonstrated not only in rat pups, but in human infants as well:

"For example, the finding that levels of growth hormone in rat pups were regulated by vigorous tactile stimulation similar to their being licked and groomed by their mothers, was translated to a clinical setting involving very low birth weight in human premature infants, by Saul Schanberg and Tiffany Field (Field et al., 1986). They found that the preemies' weight gain and overall growth while isolated in an intensive care unit could be significantly increased over a period of days by providing an intervention of stroking and limb movement...and this intervention allowed the infants to leave the intensive care unit six days earlier than a control group of infants that received traditional care." (Hofer, 2014, p. 7)

When the dams in the experiment of Skolnick et al. (1980) were prematurely separated from their own mothers, they were deprived of the hidden maternal regulators which would have, in normal circumstances, guided their development. Therefore, the dams' homeostatic processes were left unbalanced and their developmental processes were stunted. In all likelihood, their abnormal physiological development during such a critical period had significant consequences. Some of these developmental abnormalities likely affected the development of reproductive structures or epigenetic mechanisms involved in sex cell formation; either possibility, or perhaps a combination of the two, are likely to lead to mutations in the offspring which leave the offspring more vulnerable to stress ulcers; alternatively, abnormalities in the reproductive structures of the dams could lead to developmental abnormalities of the rat pups *in utero*, abnormalities which leave the pups more susceptible to stress ulcers. In other words, the findings of Skolnick et al. (1980) may be attributable to mutations in the pups induced via the developmental abnormalities of their dams (which result from the dams' loss of hidden maternal regulators), or to developmental abnormalities of the pups induced via the developmental abnormalities of their dams (which result from the dams' loss of hidden maternal regulators). These possible causes have not even been considered by Skolnick et al. (1980), nor by Hofer (2014), probably due to their ideological biases. Further research is needed—we plead that no rats are murdered if research is begun to solve this minor problem.

Claims for the importance of epigenetic inheritance "rarely exclude DNA sequence changes as the underlying cause for heritability" (Heard and Martienssen, 2014, p. 95), and Hofer (2014) fits this rule of thumb. Proponents of psychoanalysis have strong ideological motives for jumping on the neo-Lamarckian bandwagon and grossly over-exaggerating the importance of transgenerational epigenetics.

Even if transgenerational epigenetics is the culprit for the findings of Skolnick et al. (1980), it still does not mean that transgenerational epigenetics plays a major role in evolution, let alone that Lamarck was right. No soft inheritance occurs in transgenerational epigenetics. Speciation, the formation of new species, cannot occur from transgenerational epigenetic changes alone.

The concept of genetic assimilation was developed by C.H. Waddington. Waddington (1953) describes genetic assimilation thus:

"It has been suggested that if an animal is subjected to unusual circumstances to which it can adapt in a reactive manner, the development of the adaptive character might become so far canalized that it continued to appear even when the conditions returned to the previous norm." (p. 118)

Waddington proved his hypothesis through various experiments. The classic experiment of genetic assimilation, performed by Waddington, involves the canalization of bithorax *Drosophila melanogaster*. Fruit flies typically develop only one thorax. However, by exposing flies to ether early in development, Waddington induced a developmental change so that flies developed two thoraxes instead of one. Whether or not Waddington induced mutations is unclear. Next, Waddington *selected* for bithorax flies, and after the 29th generation, offspring which were not exposed to ether still expressed the bithorax phenotype. When bred together for a few generations, 70-80% of the descendants of the bithorax flies which were never exposed to ether continued to express the bithorax phenotype. (Hall, 1999, p. 157)

Just as with transgenerational epigenetics, genetic assimilation appears Lamarckian at first glance, but at first glance only. It is important to note that Waddington *selected* for the bithorax trait. Thus, genetic assimilation is a mechanism which operates *within* and *through* natural selection, and is not opposed to it. Of course, in Waddington's experiment, the selection is artificial selection, but in instances of genetic assimilation in nature, the selection which would occur (in the case that it does occur) would be natural selection. Genetic assimilation is not a case of soft inheritance.

Selecting for a trait, in this case the bithorax phenotype, whittles the gene pool down to individuals who are capable of expressing the trait, and eventually to individual whose genes favor the expression of the trait, and ultimately to individuals whose genes code for the trait. Waddington took great pains to diminish the significance of mutations in the process of genetic assimilation (Hall, 1999, p. 158). However, the more parsimonious explanation is that mutations do indeed play a large role in genetic assimilation, given the well-established role of mutations in natural selection.

To summarize genetic assimilation, as Pigliucci, Murren, and Schlichting (2006) put it: phenotypic plasticity, which is a developmental process, is shaped by natural selection, which is an evolutionary mechanism, thus resulting in genetic assimilation, which is an evolutionary *outcome* (p. 2366). We refer the reader interested in the theory of genetic assimilation to Pigliucci et al.'s essay "Phenotypic plasticity and evolution by genetic assimilation" (2006).

The foundation of modern biology is the Modern Synthesis, and since the mind is a biological organ, the foundation of empirical theories of mind must be consistent with the Modern Synthesis, which is the synthesis of natural selection, genetics, and molecular biology.

Ecology Drives Development

Haeckel's theory of recapitulation can be summed up with his phrase "ontogeny recapitulates phylogeny". Haeckel thought that an organism's development recapitulated, or re-played, its evolutionary history—in this scheme of things, development, from embryogenesis to maturation, is a fixed record of evolutionary history, a bit like fast-forwarding a VCR cassette. Haeckel's theory of recapitulation has been widely discredited—ontogeny does *not* recapitulate phylogeny—because embryos develop in different ways. Modern biologists look upon Haeckel's theory of recapitulation with contempt and disdain:

"The so-called basic law of biogenetics [Haeckel's theory of recapitulation] is wrong. No buts or ifs can mitigate this fact. It is not even a tiny bit correct or correct in a different form, making it valid in a certain percentage. It is totally wrong." (Blechschmidt, 1977, p. 32)

"Its [Haeckel's theory of recapitulation's] shortcomings have been almost universally pointed out by modern authors, but the idea still has a prominent place in biological mythology. The resemblance of early vertebrate embryos is readily explained without resort to mysterious forces compelling each individual to reclimb its phylogenetic tree." (Erlich, Holm, and Parnell, 1963, p. 66)

Despite the fundamental unsoundness of Haeckel's theory, it has continued to be employed *as if true* in psychology, especially in the study of cognitive development in children. Long before the findings of evo-devo, Margaret Mead (1931) criticized Haeckel's theory, arguing that it did not match up with the facts of cognitive development, and that the employment of Haeckel's theory in psychology was an example of ethnocentrism. Mead's (1931) findings are still highly pertinent today:

"...Mead wrote that her motivation in traveling to the South Seas was to discredit the claims that Piaget, Lévy-Bruhl, and other "structuralists" had made regarding what they called *animism* in young children's thinking...Mead reported data that she called "amazing": "In not one of the 32,000 drawings (by young 'primitive' children) was there a single case of personalization of animals, material phenomena, or inanimate objects" (Mead, 1931, p. 400). Mead parlayed these data into a tough-minded critique of Western psychology's ethnocentrism, making the point that animism and other beliefs are more likely to be culturally induced than intrinsic to early cognitive development." (Damon, 2015, p. viii)

Mead's revolutionary findings have gone largely ignored by Western psychology. Piaget, who relied as much on the theory of recapitulation as Freud, continues to be taught in the psychology classroom as if his theory of cognitive development were universal knowledge of the human mind—a clear-cut example of ethnocentrism in Western psychology and the Western educational system.

Nearly a hundred years after Mead's (1931) study, a new way to approach the relation between evolution and development exists: evolutionary developmental biology, or evo-devo. Evo-devo has grown out of findings in molecular biology, genetics, and epigenetics; whereas previously genes were conceived of solely as instructions for proteins, we now know that genes are also instructions for *how*, *when*, and *where* to build proteins, and that these "regulatory genes" regulate the timing and meta-instructions of protein construction (viz., as during embryogenesis and development (Moczeck et al., 2015, p. 201). Thus, our understanding of evolution has itself evolved and deepened; it is not only mutations which drive natural selection, but also the regulatory gene networks of development (Moczeck et al., 2015, pp. 199-200). A further consequence of this new perspective is that the organism's environment, its ecological conditions, must be recognized for its importance in driving development and evolution:

"Developmental plasticity—the ability of the genome to produce a range of phenotypes through its interactions with the environment—was once considered a special case observable in a subset of taxa, but is now recognized as the norm, and ecological conditions are recognized as being able to influence developmental outcomes at all levels of biological organization. Interactions between developing organisms and ecological circumstances therefore have the power to shape patterns of selectable variation available in a given population...At the same time, we have come to realize that developing organisms themselves shape and alter their developmental environment and ecological niche, and thus bias the selective conditions that they and descendant generations may experience..." (Moczeck et al., 2015, p. 200)

Evo-devo may be summarized in the phrase "development drives evolution". Considering the importance of ecology in shaping development, one may also say that "ecology drives development", and it follows logically that "ecology drives evolution". Evolution, after all, is driven by adaption to the environment. As it regards psychology, perhaps the most important lesson to glean from evo-devo is that "ecology drives development", that the environment shapes human development.

And, perhaps a bit redundantly, we should also remember that "development drives development", i.e., development is not a magic record of evolutionary history, rather, a child's cognitive development drives development later in human life; these later changes are sensitive to the child's initial environment (like a mathematically chaotic system).

The habitat of the human species consists largely of cultural artifacts, and these artifacts are subject to a wide range of variation—therefore, biology leads us to acknowledge the importance of culture in shaping human development: "we have come to realize that developing organisms themselves shape and alter their developmental environment and ecological niche, and thus bias the selective conditions that they and descendant generations may experience". Cultural variation means variations in ecological conditions, and these variations influence developmental outcomes. The developmental plasticity of *Homo sapiens*, especially brain plasticity and behavioral plasticity, produces a wide range of phenotypes (especially in the brain), thoughts, and behaviors through interactions with the environment, which itself is plastic (cultural plasticity). Thus, Margaret Mead's (1931) study, so out of time in her time, fits neatly with modern biology.

Physicalist Physiology

Holt (2002) writes that Freud's "borrowings of the then modish concepts of force and energy from the "biophysics movement" (sometimes misleadingly referred to as the School of Helmholtz; Cranefield, 1966) came to dominate most of his writings on metapsychology" (p. 338). The biophysics movement and the Helmholtz school are other names for physicalist physiology. Indeed, Freud's fascination with physicalist physiology explains an essential aspect of Freudian metapsychology, the "dynamic point of view" that psychic phenomena are driven by forces.

Although physicalist physiology purports to be a form of mechanistic materialism (Cranefield, 1966, pp. 35-36), it consists of little more than metaphors drawn from physics. Cranefield (1966) writes that "many workers who were strongly oriented toward the physical approach in 1850 had by 1874 turned to other methods such as those of histology" (pp. 36-37), which means that physicalist physiology was unsuccessful in its goal of describing physiology in chemical and physical terms with the methods it employed.

Upon closer examination, the purported materialism of the Helmholtz school is dubious:

"The physicalist physiologists are important to the history of morphology because part of their aim was to eject from physiology the study of form, generation, and development—aspects of life that seemed at the time essentially unmeasurable. It is through their rhetoric and the responses to it from their opponents that morphology came to be defined as a project distinct from physiology, and it is no accident that the word "morphology" appears with increasing frequency in programmatic writings from the late 1840s on." (Nyhart, 1995, p. 66)

Instead of striving to invent new ways of studying form, generation, and development, the Helmholtz school merely gave up; such a willful ignorance of material phenomena does not appear to be either scientific or materialist. The Helmholtz school was simply wrong in their assumption that the study of form, generation, and development do not belong to physiology. Indeed, advances in technology since 1847 have allowed detailed studies of a plethora of biological phenomena, form, generation, and development among them.

The three foundational concepts of metapsychology (and thus of psychoanalysis) are Lamarckian inheritance, Haeckel's theory of recapitulation, and physicalist physiology, and these three concepts are empirically wrong. No theory of mind which springs from these principles can adequately describe human behavior or psychic life. It is shocking that psychoanalysis should have had such popularity in the early half of the twentieth century given its pseudoscientific foundations, and it is dumbfounding that men and women continue to practice it in the beginning of the twenty first century. Solms's project of synthesizing neuroscience and psychoanalysis is absurd; neuroscience has as its foundation the Modern Synthesis, and is thus fundamentally incompatible with psychoanalysis.

Freud's Dynamic and Economic Points of View

By critiquing physicalist physiology, we have already provided a refutation of Freud's "dynamic point of view", which conceptualizes "motivational phenomena by the use of psychic forces". Inspired by physicalist physiology, the idea of psychic forces driving the mind's activities is a physics metaphor developed in the absence of evidence about how the brain actually functions.

It is crucial to remember that Freud's "economic point of view", the belief in "quantitative variations in amounts of psychic energies", is not quantifiable. Although the notion of "psychic energies" has become absorbed by the popular culture and folk psychology of twentieth century global (mostly Western) culture, it is scientifically meaningless. How does one go about objectively measuring psychic energy, or testing for it? Of what substance is psychic energy made? Neutrinos, quarks, dark-matter? Obviously, none of these, and neither is it made of any known form of energy in physics. Just as with the dynamic point of view, the economic view is merely a physics metaphor employed in the absence of evidence.

Holt (2002), restating common criticism of metapsychology, writes:

"Metapsychology is a closed system without links to the empirical world. Hence, its key terms cannot be measured, not even those of the economic (allegedly quantitative) point of view, and it can have no explanatory or predictive value." (p. 340)

Freud makes frequent references to "libidinal investments". As the word *investment* in this phrase implies, Freud's concept of *libido* was that of a psychic energy which is engaged in economic transactions. Although a sex drive exists in the brain, it functions very little like Freud's concept of libido. Freud's concept of libido has little to nothing to do with the biological sex drive.

Even Solms and Turnbull (2002), who are staunch advocates of integrating psychoanalysis and biology (indeed, that is the whole crux of the neuropsychoanalysis movement), even they agree that Freud's psychoanalysis is a divorce from biology:

"One hundred years ago, Freud (1900, p. 536) famously asserted that he was "disregard[ing] the fact that the apparatus with which we are here concerned is also known to us in the form of an anatomical preparation," and implored his readers to "remain upon psychological ground"...Moreover, he called only for a *period* of disciplinary independence, so that psychology may, "*for the present*...proceed according to its own requirements." Immediately he went on to add: "after we have completed our psychoanalytic work we shall have to find a point of contact with biology."" (Solms and Turnbull, 2002, pp. 297-298; the latter quote by Freud has as its source Freud, 1915, p. 175)

Of course, Solms and Turnbull are in favour of finding "a point of contact with biology". But the utility and credibility of their project is undermined by the fact, which they acknowledge, that Freud's entire project of psychoanalysis (including metapsychology) was developed only by disregarding biology. Freud strove to invent a "pure" psychology, a psychology which proceeds "according to its own requirements". Although Freud famously declared himself to be a materialist, his quest for a pure psychology is antithetical to materialist inquiry; Freud's disregard of biology (particularly of the brain), makes his metapsychology in effect a dualistic system despite its purported materialism.

Metapsychology, the theoretical foundation of psychoanalysis, proceeds as if the brain has no bearing on mental life, and this position is paradoxically described as "remaining upon psychological ground". The nineteenth century was home to several groundbreaking leaps in neuroscience, including the case of Phineas Gage, Broca's discovery of Broca's area, and Wernicke's discovery of Wernicke's area. In the wake of such discoveries, it is dumbfounding how a neurologist, Freud, can decide to invent a psychological discipline which disregards the brain. It is as if biology harboured a truth, or set of truths, which were too difficult for Freud and his followers to confront, something which made them afraid, which threatened their way of life.

Freud's Topological Point of View

Freud's "topological point of view" refers to the "structural model of ego, superego, and id". We have already extrapolated at length the inadequacy of Freud's metapsychology due to its foundations in Lamarckian inheritance, Haeckel's theory of development, and physicalist physiology. Although such concerns arise once again with the topographical point of view, there are also other serious problems with it.

The structural model of ego, superego, and id relates directly to Freud's ideas on consciousness and the unconscious mind, as well as to his ideas on child development, evolution, sexuality, civilization, and psychiatric treatment. And, as the Freudian cliché goes, it all leads back to Oedipus. In the following sections, we will deconstruct the ego, id, superego, reality principle, pleasure principle and the Oedipus complex.

A Deconstruction of the Structural Model of Ego, Id, and Superego, Part I: Contradictions and Problems of Definition

According to Freud (1923/1960), the distinction between what is conscious and what is unconscious is the basis of the operation of psychoanalysis: "Nevertheless we must beware of ignoring this characteristic, for the property of being conscious or not is in the last resort our one beacon-light in the darkness of depth psychology" (p. 8). However, what is conscious and unconscious is not well-defined in psychoanalysis; Freud's definitions of them contain many internal contradictions. Since the foundational concepts of psychoanalysis contain serious contradictions, the interpretations reached by the psychoanalytic method, which are so crucial to the "medical" practice of psychoanalysis, must contain erroneous conclusions. In other words, psychoanalysis fails to inform anyone about the thoughts and motivations of the subject. Furthermore, if the question of what is conscious and what is unconscious is approached empirically, Freud's conceptions are found to have no empirical basis, and thus the practice and theory of psychoanalysis has no empirical basis.

The psychoanalytic conception of what is conscious and unconscious depends upon Freud's hypothesis of the existence of a dynamic force which he calls *repression*:

"The state in which the ideas existed before being made conscious is called by us *repression*, and we assert that the force which instituted the repression and maintains it is perceived as *resistance* during the work of analysis. Thus we obtain our concept of the unconscious from the theory of repression." (Freud, 1923/1960, pp. 4-5)

Freud's concept of the unconscious is not only a vague entity which is "not conscious", but a dynamic force of a very particular nature. The unconscious, conceived of by Freud, is a primitive part of the mind which harbors the *Triebe*, (better translated as "drives" rather than "instincts"). Freud's vision of the mind is the same as that of folk psychology: reason represses the passions (the drives). This is also his view of civilization, whose system of punishments he views as necessary in order to repress the animal passions—and of course, he views progress as the result of successful repression (Freud, 1930/1961, pp. 46-63), a bourgeois view which legitimates socio-political repression. Modern neuroscience reveals that the dichotomy between reason and the passions is false (Damasio, 1994), therefore it is safe to conclude that society's system of punishments is not necessary to repress the "dangerous" animal passions, since the animal passions are necessary for our existence and not harmful to it, and that progress is not made by the triumph of reason over the passions. In fact, repressing the passions may have deleterious effects upon individuals and upon civilization. Wilhelm Reich, in his book *The Mass Psychology of Fascism* (1946/1980), comments extensively on the importance of anti-sex religious propaganda in Nazi ideology and the function of anti-sex religious propaganda in swaying the working class and young people to supporting the Nazi party; this pattern of religion and conservatism in conjunction with anti-sex, procreationist ideology observed by Reich frequently occurs, and is observable in the Southern states of the United States, where the Republican party and fundamentalist religious views have a stranglehold on the majority of the Anglo-American population.

Freud (1923/1960) describes consciousness as an aspect of the ego: "We have formed the idea that in each individual there is a coherent organization of mental processes; and we call this his *ego*. It is to this ego that consciousness is attached" (p. 7). Freud (1923/1960) also writes of the ego as the entity from which proceeds repression: "From this ego proceed the repressions, too, by means of which it is sought to exclude certain trends in the mind not merely from conscious but also from other forms of effectiveness and activity" (p. 7). Thus, there is an inconsistency in Freud's thought: "repression" is defined both as "the state in which the ideas existed before being made conscious" and as a force which proceeds from the ego, to which consciousness is attached.

Freud often abbreviates "unconscious" as "Ucs.", preconscious" as "Pcs.", "conscious" as "Cs.", and perception as "Pcpt.". Freud's concept of the unconscious is identified by Freud (1923/1960) as synonymous with the id:

"I propose to take into account by calling the entity which starts out from the system *Pcpt.* and begins by being *Pcs.* the 'ego', and by following Groddeck in calling the other part of the mind into which the entity extends and which behaves as though it were *Ucs.*, the 'id'." (p. 13)

However, it is central to Freud's theory that although the ego and the id are distinct, consciousness and the unconscious respectively, that they also merge into each other:

"The ego is not sharply separated from the id; its lower portion merges into it. But the repressed merges into the id as well, and is merely a part of it. The repressed is only cut off sharply from the ego by the resistances of repression; it can communicate with the ego through the id." (Freud, 1923/1960, p. 14)

This direct connection is what allows, theoretically, the unconscious to become conscious, and for conscious ideas to be repressed into the unconscious. The concept of repression is central to Freud's concepts of consciousness and the unconscious, and to the practice of psychoanalysis:

"In analysis these trends which have been shut out stand in opposition to the ego, and the analysis is faced with the task of removing the resistances which the ego displays against concerning itself with the repressed." (Freud, 1923/1960, p. 7)

If there is no basis for repression, ego, and id, then there is no basis for psychoanalysis as a medical practice. In describing the analytic situation, Freud (1923/1960) once again slips into calling a part of the ego to be conscious and another part of the ego as unconscious, despite the distinction he makes earlier that all "which behaves as though it were unconscious" (p. 13) is the id:

"Since, however, there can be no question but that this resistance emanates from his ego and belongs to it, we find ourselves in an unforeseen situation. We have come upon something in the ego itself which is also unconscious, which behaves exactly like the repressed—that is, which produces powerful effects without itself being conscious and which requires special work before it can be made conscious." (p. 7)

Within the same page, Freud then again contradicts himself by claiming that the model of a conflict between the conscious and the unconscious must be replaced by a more accurate model of conflict between the ego and the id:

"From the point of view of analytic practice, the consequence of this discovery is that we land in endless obscurities and difficulties if we keep to our habitual forms of expression and try, for instance, to derive neuroses from a conflict between the conscious and the unconscious. We shall have to substitute for this antithesis another, taken from our insight into the structural conditions of the mind—the antithesis between the coherent ego and the repressed which is split off from it." (p. 7)

So, although in Freud's *The Ego and the Id* (1923/1960) the unconscious is equated with the id (p. 13), and consciousness is equated with the ego (p. 7), repression is merged from the ego to the id (p. 14), but at the same time the ego is claimed to possess an unconscious (p. 7), and repression is not the antithesis of the conscious and the unconscious (which are identified as ego and id, respectively) but repression is the antithesis of the ego and "the repressed which is split off from it" (p. 7) at the same time as repression proceeds from the ego (p. 7). There is an obvious confusion of the meaning of terms in the founder of psychoanalysis's work, a serious error when one considers that these terms are frequently used in psychoanalysis, both in "therapy" and by the lay person.

Despite Freud (1923/1960) "calling the other part of the mind into which the entity [the ego] extends and which behaves as though it were *Ucs.*, the 'id'" (p. 13), Freud alternately, in the same work, *The Ego and the Id* (1923/1960), distinguishes between three different unconscious parts of the mind:

"Dynamic considerations caused us to make our first correction ["The latent, which is unconscious only descriptively, not in the dynamic sense, we call *preconscious*; we restrict the term *unconscious* to the dynamically unconscious repressed", p. 5]; our insight into the structure of the mind leads to the second. We recognize that the *Ucs.* does not coincide with the repressed; it is still true that all that is repressed is *Ucs.*, but not all that is *Ucs.* is repressed. A part of the ego, too—and Heaven knows how important a part—may be *Ucs.*, undoubtedly is *Ucs.* And this *Ucs.* belonging to the ego is not latent like the *Pcs.*; for if it were, it could not be activated without becoming *Cs.*" (p. 8)

The ego begins by being preconscious yet extends into the unconscious (p. 13), the preconscious and the unconscious are different entities (p. 8), while at the same time the preconscious and the unconscious are both unconscious and thus comprise the id (p. 13). Since Freud claims that the preconscious and the unconscious are distinct from each other, it is illogical to refer to them both as the id; if they are both referred to as the id, then it does not make sense to claim that they are distinct. The confusion of what the unconscious and the preconscious are, especially in relation to each other, necessarily confuses what the ego in theory is, since the definition of ego depends upon both concepts. (Freud, 1923/1960)

To add to the confusion, the repressed merges into the id and can communicate with the ego through the id (p. 14), and at the same time the unconscious does not coincide with the repressed (p. 8), and all that is repressed is unconscious (p. 8). It is uncertain whether repression, which is described as proceeding from the ego (p. 7), is unconscious or conscious, and whether the repressed does not coincide with the unconscious (thus making the repressed conscious) or all that is repressed is unconscious (p. 8). (Freud, 1923/1960)

Let us examine two statements by Freud (1923/1960) in more detail: "the *Ucs.* does not coincide with the repressed" and "all that is repressed is *Ucs.*" (p. 8). These two statements are logically contrary to each other, and thus cannot both be true as Freud claims. Freud's statements concern two central concepts to psychoanalysis: repression and the unconscious. The foundational relationship of these two concepts cannot be overstated; in Freud's own words, "the property of being conscious or not is in the last resort our one beacon-light in the darkness of depth psychology" (p. 8). Yet, when two of Freud's specific hypotheses regarding the unconscious and repression are scrutinized for logical coherence, it becomes evident that they are unable to function as Freud describes them.
Given the grievous logical errors of Freud's definitions of his key concepts, a computational model of the mind based on Freud's instructions would be unable to function. When Freud's concepts are treated as if they exist, they create irresolvable paradoxes. Since the concepts examined in this section concern the structure of the mind, and the mind is a material entity subject to the laws of nature, Freud's contradictions are "architectural errors" and his model of the structure of the mind is a mere fancy—it is socially constructed, not an empirically verifiable reality.

A Deconstruction of the Structural Model of Ego, Id, and Superego, Part II: The Tribunal of Neuroscience

By Freud's account, what is most important to psychoanalysis is the distinction between what is conscious and unconscious (1923/1960, p. 8), a distinction which in his own works Freud is unable to clearly define. In his paper "The Conscious Id", Solms (2013) defines Freud's concepts of *ego* and *id* based upon a distinction that Freud makes between two ways that the body is represented in the mind (pp. 7-9). Although this question of the body's representations does not have the privileged position to psychoanalytic theory as the question of what is conscious and unconscious, it has the advantage of being a clearly defined distinction which distinguishes ego from id. From this trivial point in Freud's metapsychology, Solms (2013) maintains that although the views of modern neuroscience turn Freudian psychoanalysis on its head, that in a way Freud was right all along (pp. 7-9). As the title of his paper, "The Conscious Id", suggests, Solms (2013) argues that it is more accurate to attribute consciousness to the id and unconsciousness to the ego.

Following Damasio (1999; 2010) and Panksepp (1998), Solms (2013) acknowledges that "core consciousness" consists of emotions generated by the body's need for homeostasis and *by the appetitive drives* (p. 7). Since one of the undisputed attributes of the id in Freud's structural model is that the id is the seat of appetitive drives, Solms (2013) argues that the "*consciousness is generated in the id*" (p. 12).

Our drives, though involuntarily active, are what we are conscious of ("I'm hungry", "I'm thirsty", "I'm sexually aroused", etc.); consciousness, at the "core" level, is how "far" or "close" we are to satisfying our drives—the closer we are to our object of desire, the more pleasure we feel, with satisfaction being the possession of the object of desire (consummation), and the further we are from our object of desire the more pain (any combination of sadness, anger, or fear) we feel. The drives are not unconscious in the Freudian sense of being active independently of consciousness and affecting consciousness without consciousness being aware of itself being affected by the drives. The drives are unconscious in the sense of being *involuntary*, and they directly produce consciousness, which, as we have already stated, is at its core an awareness of the closeness or farness of an organism to satisfying its drives. The drives produce the subject.

Damasio distinguishes "extended consciousness" from "core consciousness"; "extended consciousness" encompasses more complicated conscious cognition, including all the functions which make humans distinctly human (Damasio, 1999, pp. 195-202; Damasio, 2010). Whereas core consciousness is produced in the upper brainstem, extended consciousness is produced in the cortex; extended consciousness requires core consciousness in order to function, but core consciousness can operate in the absence of extended consciousness (Damasio, 1999; 2010).

Solms (2013) writes of an important implication of the concept of extended consciousness: "To be clear: the cortical representations are unconscious in themselves; however, when consciousness is *extended onto* them (by "attention"), they are transformed into something both conscious *and* stable, something that can be *thought* in working memory" (p. 13). In other words, representations in the cortex must be activated by core consciousness in order to become extended consciousness. However, Damasio (1999; 2010) also writes of "top-down" influence, with the associations of extended consciousness having the ability to "extend onto" and activate the emotions which are core consciousness. Since the cortex is in itself unconscious, the top-down influence can work either by the direct emotional transition of consciousness from one "idea" to another, or through the implicit activity of the cortex provoking an emotional change in consciousness.

Because Freud places the ego in the cortex, Solms (2013) identifies the cortex as the ego (pp. 7-12) and comes to the conclusion that "the ego is fundamentally unconscious" (p. 12). Of course, Solms's formulations overturns the foundational concepts of psychoanalysis. Furthermore, Solms's (2013) paper displays the inadequacy of the psychoanalytic method of arriving at knowledge of the mind, in contrast to the accurate methods of neuroscience. At first glance, it appears as if "The Conscious Id" is a big leap forward for psychoanalysis, bringing the discipline more in tune with facts. However, there is no utility in retaining the concepts *ego* and *id* because they are still too intimately linked with Freudian views of the operations of the mind, views which are empirically unfounded.

Moreover, the view of what is conscious and unconscious which is propounded by Solms (2013) discredits the basis of the "talking cure", i.e., the actual practice of psychoanalysis for the purpose of curing patients of medical illnesses.

Solms makes the distinction between two representations of the body in the brain: the "external body" and the "internal body". The external body is located in the primary somatosensory cortex and the primary motor cortex (the post-central gyrus and the pre-central gyrus, respectively), and may be described as the mind's map of the body (Solms, 2013, pp. 5-6). The internal body is located in the brainstem and plays a crucial role in homeostasis (Solms, 2013, p. 6). The external body is exteroceptive, and the internal body is interoceptive (Solms, 2013, p. 6). However, Solms (2013) introduces a contradiction, not altogether attributable to him, when he further elaborates on what he means by these two concepts:

"The internal type of consciousness consists in *states* rather than *objects* of consciousness (cf. Mesulam, 2000). The internal body is not an object of perception unless it is externalized and presented to the classical senses; it is the *subject* of perception. It is the background state of *being* conscious." (pp. 6-7)

It is problematic to describe the internal body as interoceptive and to declare that it does not become an object of perception "unless it is externalized and presented to the classical senses". For the same reason, it is problematic to describe "the internal type of consciousness", core consciousness, as consisting of states and not objects of consciousness. Furthermore, it is problematic to invoke the "classical senses", an ethnocentric conceptual framework, in this context. By definition, interoception means the *perception* of conditions within the body. Since the internal body is interoceptive, the body necessarily appears to consciousness as objects of consciousness since it is the object of perception. However, that does not necessarily preclude the internal body from simultaneously being the subject of perception and consisting of states. States of consciousness are composed of objects of consciousness.

Traditional definitions of *subject* and *object* which make clear-cut distinctions between subject and object break down when describing how subject and object are generated in the brain. Solms (2013) writes that the internal body and the external body are both representations of the body, and that core consciousness consists of representations of the internal body (pp. 5-6). A "representation" is synonymous with a "sign". The state of the internal body is also a representation of the internal body to itself; the internal body consists of an aggregate of signs. The subject is also always its own object, and both consist of signs. Affects are representations; affects, too, are aggregates of signs.

Damasio (1999) describes the biological function of emotions as twofold:

"The first function is the production of a specific reaction to the inducing situation. In an animal, for instance, the reaction may be to run or to become immobile or to beat the hell out of the enemy or to engage in pleasurable behavior...The second biological function of emotion is the regulation of the internal state of the organism such that it can be prepared for the specific reaction." (pp. 53-54; emphasis my own)

Emotions, and the drives which produce them, are not cut off from the world. Emotions and drives are in constant interaction with the environment external to the organism. Emotions are not only the "core" of being, they are also being-in-the-world, because being always means being in the world. Emotions function to induce real, concrete actions of the subject in re-action to its environment. Damasio's point neatly synthesizes affective neuroscience, the neuroscience of subjectivity, with behavioral science, which has long ignored subjectivity, because emotions (and thus consciousness) are the basis on which associative learning is able to occur. Damasio (1999) hints at this synthesis:

"At their most basic, emotions are part of homeostatic regulation and are poised to avoid the loss of integrity that is a harbinger of death or death itself, as well as to endorse a source of energy, shelter, or sex. And as a result of powerful learning mechanisms such as conditioning, emotions of all shades eventually help connect homeostatic regulation and survival "values" to numerous events and objects in our autobiographical experience." (p. 54)

The view of emotions and drives as evolutionary adaptions is at odds with Freud's view of the id (the drives) as magically isolated from reality: "The id, cut off from the external world, has a world of perception of its own" (Freud, 1940, p. 198, as quoted in Solms, 2013, p. 8). It is on the basis of an unconscious cut off from reality that Freud develops the idea that the id and the ego are fundamentally opposed to each other, the id being governed by the pleasure principle and the ego being governed by the reality principle:

"Moreover, the ego seeks to bring the influence of the external world to bear upon the id and its tendencies, and endeavours to substitute the reality principle for the pleasure principle which reigns unrestrictedly in the id. For the ego, perception plays the part which in the id falls to instinct. The ego represents what may be called reason and common sense, in contrast to the id, which contains the passions. All this falls into line with popular distinctions which we are all familiar with; at the same time, however, it is only to be regarded as holding good on the average or 'ideally'." (Freud, 1923/1960, p. 15)

According to Freud himself, one of the central ideas of psychoanalysis is reducible to a platitude of folk psychology, that reason and emotion ("the passions") are opposed to each other. Freud's concepts of the pleasure principle and the reality principle are merely extensions of this platitude. Freud cautions that the opposition between reason and emotion is true only "on the average or 'ideally'". However, Damasio's (1994) book *Descartes' Error: Emotion, Reason, and the Human Brain* is devoted in its entirety to proving that the popular opposition of folk psychology between reason and emotion is a false dichotomy:

"The strategies of human reason probably did not develop, in either evolution or any single individual, without the guiding force of the mechanisms of biological regulation, of which emotion and feeling are notable expressions. Moreover, even after reasoning strategies become established in the formative years, their effective deployment probably depends, to a considerable extent, on a continued ability to experience feelings...This is not to deny that emotions and feelings can cause havoc in the processes of reasoning under certain circumstances...It is thus even more surprising and novel that the absence of emotion and feeling is no less damaging, no less capable of compromising the rationality that makes us distinctively human and allows us to decide in consonance with a sense of personal future, social convention, and moral principle." (p. xli)

"The passions", i.e. the appetitive drives, are not cut off from the external world and opposed to the organism's sense of reality. To the contrary, the drives are in constant interaction with the world and are essential to the organism's sense of reality. The impairment of emotions, which means the impairment of states produced by drives, impairs the individual's ability to think rationally, i.e. to interact with the real world.

For the same reason there is no ego, there is no superego. Morality, too, is dependent upon the emotions and thus upon the drives—whether one is discussing ethical decision-making or the learned associations which serve as the basis for ethical decision-making. Damasio (1994) inadvertently proves that all morality is subjective and culturally relative because of his finding that morality is dependent upon emotions; emotions are a highly subjective phenomenon, and each culture indoctrinates its members with a set of morals by associating certain ideas and images with emotional states (viz. through cultural artifacts such as stories, music, art, religion, science, etc., as well as by rituals and child-rearing practices).

The fact of the culturally relative nature of morality directly contradicts Freud's theories of a Lamarckian genealogy of morality and guilt—the Oedipus complex as Original Sin:

"In *Totem and Taboo*, for example, Freud argued that the Oedipus complex has its origins in a single historical event, which he claimed took place in prehistory. According to Freud, a 'band of brothers' at one point rose up to kill their father, in order to gain sexual access to their mother and sisters. Overcome by guilt, they made a taboo out of the reason behind their patricide; this guilt, in turn, gave rise to the practice of what Freud referred to as *totemism*. What makes

Freud's usage of this hypothetical scenario Lamarckian is that he claimed that the memory of this event, along with the accompanying guilt, was inherited by subsequent generations, up until the present day. The reason we don't all have access to this memory, according to Freud, is because each and every one of us represses it; nevertheless, it lies ready to hand in the unconscious of all human beings, and has influenced the way our cultures have taken shape, particularly in the case of religion." (Rensma, 2013, p. 262)

This wild speculation of Freud's is a just-so story which merely reinforces the ethnocentric bourgeois ideals of his society. Freud, in effect, attempts to legitimate the Original Sin by claiming for it a historical basis and localizing it in the brain. Neither do we genetically inherit guilt from "the sins of the father", nor do we genetically inherit moral values. Furthermore, no taboo is universal, not even the incest taboo. Incest *avoidance* occurs in nature, but mechanisms of incest avoidance only work *statistically*, and animals are fundamentally unaware of kinship ties and the fact that sexual activity facilitates reproduction; indeed, humans too are born unaware that sexual activity facilitates reproduction, even we need to *learn* the "facts of life", especially the specific mechanisms of reproduction (which were not even fully known until the twentieth century). Furthermore, incest avoidance, because it is a natural mechanism, occurs spontaneously (when it occurs) and is not reinforced by social and cultural means—the incest *taboo*, on the other hand, *is* reinforced by social and cultural means. As Maurice Godelier demonstrates in his book *The Metamorphoses of Kinship* (2004/2012), the incest taboo is culturally relative, it is not present ubiquitously in all cultures. Furthermore, it is not "backwards" or "primitive" civilizations which have historically practiced "incest" (where there is no incest taboo, the term "incest" no longer applies), but highly culturally and technologically advanced civilizations, such as Ancient Egypt (their royalty, no less) and Achaemenid Persia (Godelier, 2004/2012; Goody, 2005, p. 129). Therefore, "in face of the facts of history, which show that brother-sister, father-daughter and mother-son relations have in some societies, such as Ancient Egypt or Achaemenid Persia, *not only not been prohibited, but even enjoined*" (Goody, 2005, p. 129; my own emphasis), we must conclude that the incest taboo does not have a biological origin, that it is not ingrained in "human nature" (if such a thing as "human nature" even exists, which is doubtful), and that the incest taboo is not a universal categorical imperative.

Damasio's (1994) view that reason and morality are dependent upon emotions is supported by neuroscience research, including his own and his colleagues' widely acknowledged and celebrated research. The work of Damasio and his colleagues shows that when the capacity to feel emotions is damaged, the ability to reason is also damaged, suggesting that rationality is dependent upon emotions, and thus upon the drives.

An experiment known as the Iowa Gambling Task explores the extent to which rational choices depend upon emotions. In the Iowa Gambling Task, subjects can draw one card at a time from four different packs of cards. Certain packs are riskier than others because they result in more net losses; on the other hand, other packs are safer and yield more rewards. Subjects are not told which pack is which, or that there is a difference between packs. The subjects must discover the risks and rewards of each pack by trial and error. Subjects with relatively healthy brains initially experiment with all four decks, but over time begin to show signs of nervous tension when selecting cards from the risky decks and shift their preferences towards the safe decks. Subjects with damage to the prefrontal cortex or the amygdala, both of which are key to the processing of emotional stimuli, show no signs of nervous tension when picking cards from the risky decks and they continue choosing the risky decks. The ability to feel emotions facilitates the emotional learning necessary to make decisions which benefit the self, i.e., emotions are necessary to make rational choices. (Bechara, Damasio, Damasio, and Lee, 1999)

It is important to note that although Damasio (1994) describes "the absence of emotion and feeling" as damaging to reason (p. xli), that his dysfunctional subjects do not, in the strict sense, have a total absence of emotion and feeling. It is more accurate to say that they have *impairments* of emotion and feeling. Consistent with Damasio's (2010) and Panksepp's (1998) hypothesis that consciousness is an emotional state generated by the brainstem, patients who have damage to the prefrontal cortex as described in *Descartes' Error* are still able to feel, albeit in a diminished way and often only to a narrow range of stimuli. One of Damasio's patients,

Elliot, although calm, detached, and "emotionless" the majority of the time, would on rare occasions become angry, although his outbursts were swift and he would become calm again quickly and hold no grudges (Damasio, 1994, p. 45). Moreover, Damasio (1994) does not report any impairments of primitive homeostatic affects which are necessary for body regulation in Elliot, nor does he report impairments of nociception (a condition known as congenital insensitivity to pain, or CIP).

Whereas in Anglo folk psychology and Anglo academic psychology, emotions tend to be viewed as aberrations which are "departures" from the "normal state", emotion as something to be controlled and suppressed, emotion as a disruption to the organization of life—in traditional Russian culture, the perspective on emotions is quite different:

"On the other hand, there is ample evidence showing that, for example, from the point of view of traditional Russian culture, states such as "joy", "worry", "sadness", "sorrow", "grief", "delight", and so on constitute most people's normal state, and that an absence of "emotions" would be seen as indicating a deadening of a person's *duša* ("heart/soul"). In fact, experiences comparable to "joy", "sadness", or "anger" are often conceptualized in Russian as inner activities in which one engages rather than as states which one passively undergoes, and so they are often designated by verbs rather than adjectives. Some examples: *radovat'sja* "to rejoice" (in English archaic), *grustit'* (from *grust'*, roughly "sadness"), *toskovat'* (from *toska* "melancholy-cum-longing"), *serdit'sja* (roughly, "to be angry", but a verb, like *to rage* in English), *stydit'sja* (roughly "to be ashamed"), and so on...The cultural ideal of "composure" as a person's "normal state" is alien to mainstream Russian culture..." (Wierzbicka, 1999, pp. 17-18)

The perspective of traditional Russian culture is supported by Damasio's (1994; 1999; 2010) research; a complete absence of emotion does indeed mean death for the organism and thus the psyche (the *duša*), and a relative absence of emotion, such as happens in cases of lesions to the vmPFC, also comes with a "deadening" of the psyche, an absence of motivation, passion, and rational decision-making. Moreover, the traditional Russian perspective is echoed by sociology: it is with and through the "inner activity" of emotions in which we are engaged that we construct, or socially construct, the reality of everyday life, due to cultural indoctrination which associates certain ideas and images with certain feelings. It is in Russia, in the midst of the perspective of traditional Russian culture, that emotions are the core of life by which we actively construct our reality, that the great psychologists were born and nurtured: Dostoevsky, Chekhov, Gogol, Tolstoy, Nabokov.

But Freud would not have had to look so far in order to find a different perspective on emotions. Goethe, too, at least in the following couplet, conceived of emotions as the very substance of life:

"Die uns das Leben gaben, herrliche Gefühle
Erstarren in dem irdischen Gewühle.

The fine emotions whence our lives we mold
Lie in the earthly tumult dumb and cold."
(*Faust*, Pt.1, sc.1, 1.286; as quoted in Wierzbicka, 1999, p. 18)

Wierzbicka's (1999) commentary on the above lines reveals the meaning of the original German: "From Goethe's point of view, *herrliche Gefühle* ("glorious feelings") are not something that has to be controlled or something that threatens to impair, or interfere with, "organized behavior"; rather, they are positive forces that "give us life"" (p. 18). Poets and artists, too, are often trapped in the symbolic universe of their sociocultural milieu—but on occasion, as this fragment by Goethe reveals, they have the capacity to move beyond the limits of society and culture in order to arrive at a fragment of truth, a movement which parallels that of scientists and mathematicians.

A long, long history of Western thought conserves the false dichotomy between reason and emotion (or what amounts to the same thing, the false dichotomy between reason and passion), from the Stoics to Christ to Descartes to Kant to Western psychology textbooks. The dichotomy of reason and emotion, or reason and passion, is false even when considered on the average. On the average, the ability to reason is vitally dependent upon the ability to feel emotions, which are produced by the passions. Freud, in conserving the false dichotomy between reason and emotion in his concepts of the ego and the id (and their corresponding "principles", the reality principle and the pleasure principle, respectively), upholds an ancient, ethnocentric tradition of Western folk psychology. In reality, the emotions, and the "passions" or drives which they are dependent upon, mediate the relationship of the organism with its environment (reality). In his book *Looking for Spinoza: Joy, Sorrow, and the Feeling Brain* (2003), Damasio reflects more upon the nuanced relationship between emotion, passion, and reason.

Freud's concepts of the ego and the id (and by implication the reality principle and the pleasure principle), are fundamentally unsupported by empirical evidence. In other words, the concepts *ego*, *id*, *reality principle*, and *pleasure principle* are social constructs; such concepts cannot reasonably serve as the basis for understanding the human mind, a conceptual framework to understand neuroscience, a conceptual framework to understand civilization, as tools in the clinical practice of psychotherapy, or as guides for the attainment of happiness.

In the history of psychoanalytic literature and works inspired by psychoanalysis, the concepts of *ego* and *id* will remain as confused as Freud's own usage, but perhaps oversimplified, according to Freud's own directions, to mean *ego=consciousness* and *id=unconscious*. Faced with the overwhelming historical usage of these terms, Solms's reinvention of Freud's structural model is futile. Moreover, the ultimate basis of the concepts of *ego* and *id* are untenable, therefore simply changing an aspect of their meaning (*id=consciousness* and *ego=unconscious*) is trivial, for it does not address the fact that the basis of these concepts rests upon social constructs and not empirical evidence.

Metapsychology is wrong from both the Solmsian and the Freudian points of view. Revising the concepts of the ego and the id is a trivial pursuit. Not only are Freud's concepts based upon obsolete hypotheses such as Lamarckian inheritance and physicalist physiology, but in addition, Freud's concepts are internally inconsistent and they are unsupported by the findings of contemporary neuroscience. We have seen, in turn, how Freud's metapsychology, both in general and in the specific contents of its dynamic, economic, and topographic (or structural) points of view, is false.

We need new concepts in order to understand the mind, or perhaps old ones buried in the philosophies of other cultures.

Attachment and Sexual Desire Are Controlled By Different Brain Mechanisms

The formula of the Oedipus complex is simple and popularly known: the male child sexually desires his own mother and develops resentment for his father due to his sexual jealousy. It is from the Oedipus complex that the id, ego, and superego are formed (Freud, 1923/1960, pp. 18-29). Oedipus is the very foundation of psychoanalysis itself, from which its metapsychology and therapeutic practice find their justification. The burden of proof falls upon psychoanalysis to prove the existence of the Oedipus complex, and to date, no hard evidence has been furnished. To the contrary, positive evidence has been furnished that the Oedipus complex does not exist.

According to Freud (1923/1960), the Oedipus complex proceeds in the following way:

"At a very early age the little boy develops an object cathexis for his mother, which originally related to the mother's breast and is the prototype of an object-choice on the anaclitic model; the boy deals with his father by identifying himself with him. For a time these two relationships proceed side by side, until the boy's sexual wishes in regard to his mother become more intense and his father is perceived as an obstacle to them; from this the Oedipus complex originates. His identification with his father then takes on a hostile colouring and changes into a wish to get rid of his father in order to take his place with his mother. Henceforward his relation to his father is ambivalent; it seems as if the ambivalence inherent in the identification from the beginning had become manifest. An ambivalent attitude to his father and an object-relation of a solely affectionate kind to his mother make up the content of the simple positive Oedipus complex in a boy." (pp. 21-22)

The central idea in the Oedipus complex is the child's sexual desire for the mother, upon which the jealous desire to murder the father depends. However, the nature of the child's bond to the mother is *attachment*, which is a neurologically distinct system from the sex drive; this is a fact which Solms and Turnbull (2002) are well aware of, since they present the work of Panksepp (1998) on the subject.

According to Panksepp (1998), there are four "basic-emotion command systems" in the brain: SEEKING, RAGE, FEAR, and PANIC. Although Panksepp (1998) uses all-caps in writing of these systems, we will abandon the all-caps convention as it serves no utility and it is a typographical eye-sore. The sex drive operates through the seeking system. The panic system is the inverse dimension of the attachment system; the "attachment system" as such is not described by Panksepp (1998), but it is safe to infer its nature from the data presented.

When need-detector mechanisms in the hypothalamus detect a deficient level of biologically primal needs, the seeking system is activated (Solms and Turnbull, 2002, p. 117). These biologically primal, or primordial, needs include hunger, thirst, and sex: "This system is heavily activated during sexual arousal and other appetitive states...There is also a thirst detector, a hunger detector, even a "sexual-need" detector" (Solms and Turnbull, 2002, pp. 116-117). The "command neurotransmitter" of the seeking system is dopamine, and it forms part of the meso-cortical-mesolimbic DA system (Solms and Turnbull, 2002, p. 116). The seeking system, also known as the reward system, "promotes exploratory behavior" (Solms and Turnbull, 2002, p. 115). Although the DA system also serves the function of a "fear system", as we shall see in a later section, let us for now limit our discussion of the DA system to its function as a "seeking system".

Confusingly, Panksepp (1998) describes the system responsible for the gratification and consummation of appetites as the LUST subsystem (a subsystem of the seeking system). Here, we retain the all-caps because Panksepp's use of the word "lust" differs greatly from its generally accepted meaning. "Lust" is generally taken to mean sexual desire, and not necessarily the consummation of sexual desire. Therefore, "LUST subsystem" is a highly misleading name; it is much more accurate to describe it as the *consummation system* or *subsystem*, especially since its function "on the motor side...switches appetitive behaviors off and replaces them with consummatory behaviors" (Solms and Turnbull, 2002, p. 119). The seeking system more accurately represents lust as it is commonly understood: the sex drive. By contrast, the consummation system is best characterized as "instinctual behavior patterns [which] are automatically released when the object of a biological need is attained" (Solms and Turnbull, 2002, p. 119). The command neurotransmitter for the consummation system is endorphin (Solms and Turnbull, 2002, p. 120). The consummation subsystem depends upon the seeking system for activation, but the seeking system does not depend upon the consummation subsystem for activation: the consummation of desire can only take place if there is desire, but desire is not always consummated.

The panic system, also called the separation-distress system and the grief system, plays an important role in social bonding, parenting, and development, and is first (potentially) activated in the infant when the infant is separated from its primary caregiver (Solms and Turnbull, 2002, pp. 129-131). The command neurotransmitters of the panic system are opioids, but oxytocin and prolactin also play important roles in it (Solms and Turnbull, 2002, p. 130). Although the seeking system operates independently of the panic system, the panic system, at least initially, stimulates the seeking system:

"Sustained stimulation of [the panic system] in freely roaming animals produces an interesting sequence of behaviors. Initially, when the system is first stimulated, it promotes [seeking] behaviors, together with distress vocalizations. Presumably this increases the chances of finding the mother, or of being found. After a more or less set period of time, there is a change to *withdrawal* from the environment as the animal retreats into isolation and displays a sort of hibernation behavior that looks for all the world like depression." (Solms and Turnbull, 2002, p. 130-131)

In the above quoted passage, Solms and Turnbull (2002) are of course recapitulating the findings of Bowlby (1969) on attachment, rephrasing Bowlby's (1969) finding of the "biphasic protest-despair response" of separation in Pankseppian terminology. Solms and Turnbull (2002) also comment on the inverse dimension of the panic system, attachment:

"The role played by endogenous opioids in [the panic system] teaches us an interesting lesson about the nature of attachment...Here, the animal receives *constant* reinforcement, and inappropriate behaviors are associated with the *withdrawal* of this reinforcement. It is this type of schedule that appears to govern the separation-distress system." (p. 131)

The panic system is essentially an opioid withdrawal mechanism which evolved by natural selection in order to increase the infant's chances of survival. The panic system is the inverse dimension of the attachment system because the panic system only becomes activated when the individual is separated from its attachment figure. Therefore, we can infer that the attachment system is an opioid addiction: "the animal receives *constant* reinforcement". In other words, the attachment bond to the attachment figure (the primary caregiver) is maintained by a feeling of bliss produced by opioids released in the brain in the presence of the attachment figure. The panic system, more properly, is a subsystem of the attachment system, and it is the attachment system as such that deserves to be merited the status of a "basic-emotion command system", since the panic system only becomes activated when the attachment system "turns off". Therefore, the four basic emotion-command systems in the brain are: SEEKING, RAGE, FEAR, and ATTACHMENT.

Since the activation of the panic system is induced by opioid deprivation, it is perhaps more accurate to ascribe its command neurotransmitters to the attachment system (opiods, oxytocin, and prolactin; the latter two are involved in social bonding among other things).

Thus, it is now apparent that there is a physiological difference between the sex drive and attachment, and that the nature of the child's bond with its primary caregiver is an attachment bond, not a sexual relationship. Since the child's bond to the mother is an attachment bond and not sexual desire, the empirical evidence refutes Freud's concept of the Oedipus complex.

If a child does indeed have resentment or an ambivalent attitude towards his father, it is not due to sexual jealousy. A more parsimonious explanation of a child's resentment or ambivalent attitude towards his father is that the father has ill-treated the child. The research of Straus, Douglas, and Medeiros (2014) demonstrates that corporal punishment weakens the child-to-parent bond and that "even when used by highly supportive parents, spanking is linked to a weakened bond and higher delinquency" (p. 120). Corporal punishment was much more common in Europe during Freud's lifetime, and he may have overlooked its importance in the father-child (as well as mother-child) relationship because it was an accepted, even encouraged, norm of his society.

As Deleuze and Guattari (1972/1977) point out, Freud's analysis of the Schreber case completely ignores the sadistic character of Schreber's father, who, it was discovered in 1959 by W.G. Niederland, invented torture devices for children in the name of morality: "for example head straps with a metallic shank and leather bands, for restrictive use on children, for making them straighten up and behave" (p. 297). In making the origin of resentment towards the father endogenous to the child's psyche, Freud blames the victim.

Attachment is Independent of Orality in Infants

To further clarify the difference between the attachment bond and the sexual relationship between mother and son described by Freud, it is necessary to examine specific claims made by Freud and compare them to the findings of experimental psychology.

According to Bowlby (1969), Freud developed an influential view in psychoanalysis, dominant in his writing until his very last works, that the libido begins by being auto-erotic with the exception of the baby finding the mother's breast as its first sexual object (pp. 361-362). This is, of course, the oral stage. In the oral stage, the dominant sexual organ of the infant is the mouth, and the infant's sexual desire for the mother is expressed with the mouth (through suckling on the breast). However, the infant's orality has been demonstrated to be related to hunger and not sex.

Freud's idea of the oral stage as a sexual stage is deeply related to his other views of the mother-infant bond. According to Bowlby (1969, p. 362), Freud wrote in *The Interpretation of Dreams* (1900) that "when people are absent, children do not miss them with any great intensity; many mothers have learnt this to their sorrow", a passage which remained even in later editions of the work (*S.E.*, 4, p. 255). Bowlby's (1969) experimental work in attachment theory demonstrates that infants do indeed experience anxiety when separated from their mothers.

Bowlby (1969) goes on to point out that Freud also held the opposite view, that children do miss their mothers when they are absent (p. 363). Freud wrote:

"The reason why the infant in arms wants to perceive the presence of its mother is only because it already knows by experience that she satisfies all its needs without delay. The situation, then, which it regards as a 'danger' and against which it wants to be safeguarded is that of non-satisfaction, of a *growing tension due to need*, against which it is helpless." (*Inhibitions, Symptoms and Anxiety*, *S.E.*, 20, pp. 137-138; as quoted in Bowlby, 1969)

The "needs" of the infant that Freud refers to is not only hunger and thirst, but also sexual desire, an obvious fact if taken in context of his work, especially on the oral stage mentioned above.

For Freud, the infant's nourishment—its behavior of suckling—is inseparably linked to the child's sexual desire for the mother. For Freud, orality defines the early mother-child bond.

Harlow and Zimmerman (1959) describe hypotheses such as Freud's "drive reduction theory":

"This theory proposes that the infant's attachment to the mother results from the association of the mother's face and form with the alleviation of certain primary drive states, particularly hunger and thirst. Thus, through learning, affection becomes a self-supporting, derived drive." (p. 421)

Of course, for Freud, the mother-child bond was also motivated by the desire to alleviate the sex drive. In psychoanalytic jargon, the energy of the child's libido increases over time, building up pressure which seeks to be discharged; in this case the discharge takes the form of sucking the mother's breast for nourishment and erotic pleasure.

To test competing hypotheses of the child-to-mother bond, Harlow and Zimmerman used rhesus macaques; because they are primates and display similar bonds to their mothers, and for a few other reasons, rhesus macaques were chosen as model organisms. The monkeys were separated from their mother 6 to 12 hours after birth to be raised in the laboratory and used in experiments. In varying experimental conditions, the monkeys received one or both of two possible surrogate mothers: a cloth-mother made of terry cloth and a wire-mother made of wire. Depending on the experimental condition, bottles were attached to either one or both or none of the surrogate mothers. (Harlow and Zimmerman, 1959, pp. 421-423)

Terry cloth, or cheesecloth, was used in the construction of one surrogate mother because:

"In the course of raising these infants we observed that they all showed a strong attachment to the cheesecloth blankets which were used to cover the wire floors of their cages. Removal of these cloth blankets resulted in violent emotional behavior. These responses were not short-lived; indeed, the emotional disturbance lasted several days, as was indicated by the infant's refusal to work on the standard learning tests that were being conducted at the time. Similar observations had already been made by Foley and by van Wagenen, who stressed the importance of adequate contact responses to the very survival of the neonatal macaque." (Harlow and Zimmerman, 1959, p. 422)

The infant macaques' behavior towards the terry cloth is consistent with the behavior of mammals towards their primary caregiver in the wild. As mentioned in the previous section, infants remain in close contact with their primary caregiver, and when separated they produce distress signals and at first explore the environment in search of their primary caregiver, then withdraw from the world and become depressed. The parallel with the behavior of the macaques towards a mere cheesecloth blanket which lines their floors is astonishing. When the cloth was removed, the infants displayed "violent emotional behavior", which likely included distress vocalizations. Due to spatial limitations of the environment of the cage, exploratory behavior could obviously not have been observed. However, depression in the macaques was observed: the infants were unable to work on the standard learning tests of the researchers, reminiscent of the inability to work or attend school which often results from depression. It is important to note that at this stage, there is no artificial surrogate mother, only a cheesecloth blanket, suggesting that attachment in primates is dependent on physical contact. Harlow and Zimmerman (1959) label the role of physical contact in attachment "contact comfort" (p. 423).

In one experiment, both surrogate mothers were placed in the infant monkey's cage, in separate cubicles. The variable of nursing—of nourishment—was the independent variable. One group was wire-fed: only the wire-mother contained a bottle for nursing. The other group was cloth-fed: only the cloth-mother contained a bottle for nursing. In both groups, the infant macaques showed a distinct preference for the cloth-mother; they spent the majority of their day with the cloth-mother, whether or not the cloth-mother fed them. The experiment was conducted over 165 days. After an adjustment period of 21-25 days, the infant macaques in both groups spent on average more than 15 hours of the day with the cloth-mother for the remaining ~140 days, and on average less than 3 hours per day with the wire-mother for the remaining ~140 days. (Harlow and Zimmerman, 1959, pp. 422-423)

On the implication of the above finding as it relates to the competing hypothesis of Freud, Harlow and Zimmerman (1959) write:

"These data make it obvious that contact comfort is a variable of critical importance in the development of affectional responsiveness to the surrogate mother, and that nursing appears to play a negligible role. With increasing age and opportunity to learn, an infant fed from a lactating wire mother does not become more responsive to her, as would be predicted from a derived-drive theory, but instead becomes increasingly more responsive to its nonlactating cloth mother. These findings are at complete variance with a drive-reduction theory of affectional development." (p. 423)

The above experiment alone demonstrates the non-existence of "orality" as conceived of by Freud. The fact that the macaques spent a minimal amount of time with the wire-mother when the wire-mother was "lactating" suggests that the rooting instinct and nursing are motivated by the hunger-drive; their preference for the cloth-mother regardless of whether the cloth-mother was lactating suggests that the child-to-parent bond is independent of the hunger-drive. In Freud's concept of orality, the hunger-drive and the sex drive are fused and it is this fusion which characterizes the child-to-mother bond of the early infant. Since the hunger-drive and the child-to-mother bond operate independently of each other in the infants, it is clear that there is no sexual desire for the mother being expressed orally; the infant's bond to the mother is not oral in its nature, and the "oral" activity of nursing does not induce a stronger social bond in the infant.

To further demonstrate that the bond to the cloth-mother was one of attachment, Harlow and Zimmerman (1959) invoked fear and distress in the infant monkeys with a fear stimulus, a doll of an upright, walking bear wearing striped pants held up by suspenders and playing a toy drum—a children's toy with wide open, unblinking, and inhuman eyes (p. 423). In both wire-fed and cloth-fed conditions, the infants, when presented with the fear stimulus, ran and clung to the cloth-mother (Harlow and Zimmerman, 1959, p.

423). After running to the cloth-mother, infants lost their fear rapidly:

"Indeed, within a minute or two most of the babies were visually exploring the very thing which so shortly before had seemed an object of evil. The bravest of the babies would actually leave the mother and approach the fearful monsters, under, of course, the protective gaze of their mothers." (Harlow and Zimmerman, 1959, p. 423)

In a different experimental condition, Harlow and Zimmerman (1959) examined the response to the fear stimulus in monkeys which had been raised only with a lactating wire-mother (p. 424). When presented with the fear stimulus, the wire-fed monkeys retreated to the wire-mother, but they were not comforted by the wire-mother:

"The infants raised on the wire mother, on the other hand, rushed away from the feared object toward their mother but did not cling to or embrace her. Instead, they would either clutch themselves and rock and vocalize for the remainder of the test or rub against the side of the cubicle. Contact with the cubicle or the mother did not reduce the emotionality produced by the introduction of the fear stimulus." (Harlow and Zimmerman, 1959, p. 424)

Even in the absence of a competing surrogate mother, the lactating wire-mother, which nourishes the infant without providing contact comfort, fails to induce an attachment bond in the baby macaque. This definitively disproves Freud's hypothesis that the child's bond to the mother depends upon nourishment and it definitively disproves his hypothesis that the child-to-mother bond is a sexual relationship which finds consummation in the oral sucking behavior of the infant during nursing.

Although Freud tends to overemphasize the mother's breasts when discussing the oral stage, he did not consider the oral stage to hold true for breast-fed babies only; according to Freud himself, the oral stage and Oedipus take their course whether the infant is breast-fed or bottle-fed:

"...the phylogenetic foundation has so much the upper hand over personal accidental experience that it makes no difference whether a child has really sucked at the breast or has been brought up on the bottle and never enjoyed the tenderness of a mother's care. In both cases the child's development takes the same path..." (Freud, *An Outline of Psychoanalysis*, 1940, *S.E.*, 23, p. 188; as quoted in Bowlby, 1969, p. 364)

Thus, Harlow and Zimmerman's (1959) experiments, in which the infant macaques receive nourishment from a bottle in varying experimental conditions, do indeed concern Freud's concepts of orality and child development. Since Freud posits his hypotheses on development have a strong "phylogenetic foundation", one would expect them to hold true, if they are true at all, in other primate species. However, as we have demonstrated, Freud's hypotheses have been proven false.

According to Freud, the function of physical contact in the mother-child bond is sexual seduction; by touching the child, the mother seduces the child:

"The first object is later completed into the person of the child's mother, who not only nourishes it but also looks after it and thus arouses in it a number of other physical sensations, pleasurable and unpleasurable. By her care of the child's body she becomes its first seducer. In these two relations lies the root of a mother's importance..." (Freud, *An Outline of Psychoanalysis*, 1940, *S.E.*, 23, p. 188; as quoted in Bowlby, 1969, p. 364)

Although we have already seen how attachment and the sex drive are controlled by different brain mechanisms, let us examine more closely Freud's hypothesis and evidence which disproves his hypothesis.

As we have written in a previous passage, Hofer and his colleagues, who have studied attachment and development in rat pups, include physical contact among a list of "hidden maternal regulators", and hidden maternal regulators have been found in human infants as well; physical contact in the mother-child relationship helps maintain homeostasis and promote development in the infant.

Physical contact in the mother-child relationship has a two-fold function: by inducing an attachment bond in the infant it keeps the infant near the mother and thus safe from predators, and it promotes the release of growth hormones necessary for the infant's development. The observation of Foley and van Wagenen, "who stressed the importance of adequate contact responses to the very survival of the neonatal macaque" (Harlow and Zimmerman, p. 422), applies to a wide range of species, probably to all mammals and perhaps to some avian species.

By touching the child, the mother is not seducing the child. Whether the mother is aware of it or not, by touching her child the mother is regulating her child's physiology and stimulating the child's physiological development; this is a vital biological function of physical contact, and by extension, a vital biological function of the attachment bond.

Anoedipal Infantile Sexuality

Let us be clear about our position: we are not social conservatives who claim that children are asexual "pure" beings completely devoid of sexual desire or sexual behavior. Our position, rather, is that sexuality, including infantile sexuality, is primarily social, i.e., non-oedipal, or anoedipal—in other words, non-familial—and that Oedipus is imposed upon the individual by psychoanalysis, a process which Deleuze and Guattari (1972/1977) call *oedipalization*. Even when the infant's sexual behavior is directed towards the mother, it is an anoedipal desire. By contrast, Freud believed in an infantile sexuality that was primarily familial in nature, a sexuality that legitimates taboo (the father prevents the child's incestuous sexual wish for the mother from becoming consummated), and thus a sexuality which is in its essence taboo, since it is built upon taboo and all subsequent sexual desires lead back to incest and the prohibition of incest. Sex as the dirty little secret—an open secret, but a dirty secret nonetheless.

Our above conclusions concerning the socially constructed nature of Freud's concepts of the ego and the id support our hypothesis that infantile sexuality is primarily non-familial and anoedipal. According to Freud's hypothesis, the Oedipus complex leads to the development of the ego, id, and superego; since these concepts are social constructs and not empirically valid, their source, the Oedipus complex, is also a social construct, not an empirical reality. However, to make a thorough argument, we shall also examine infantile sexuality and contrast it with Freud's hypotheses. Lewis (1965), with the purpose of legitimating the Oedipus complex, wrote on the observance of pelvic thrust movements in human infants, beginning at eight to ten months of age:

"In a moment of apparent delight, the child clasps the mother, perhaps while relaxed on her breast. Throwing his arms about her neck, nuzzling her chin, he begins rapid rotating pelvic thrusts at a frequency of about two per second. This does not last long (10-15 seconds). It is not usually accompanied by erection...and does not result in anything suggesting orgasm...It is not restricted to boys. The mother of three girls observed it in all her daughters...It does not occur in connection with feeding, dressing or active play, although occasionally thrusting has been seen when the child is in relaxed ventral contact with a blanket or pillow." (as quoted in Bowlby, 1969, p. 158)

To begin, it is important to note that pelvic thrusting in infants does not occur in connection with feeding, which contradicts Freud's hypothesis that sexuality in infants is first expressed through orality and the taking of nourishment.

A second detail to which attention must be brought, or rather brought back to, is that attachment and sexual desire are controlled by different brain mechanisms; in other words, the child's sexual behavior towards the mother (if there is any) *occurs independently of the attachment bond.* For Freud, as we have repeatedly mentioned, the child's bond to the mother is due to the child's sexual desire for the mother—the facts, however, show that the child's bond to the mother is one of attachment. Furthermore, attachment is not dependent upon sexual desire, and sexual desire is not dependent upon attachment. Even if a child has sexual desire for his mother, this sexual desire is not the basis of his bond with his mother.

Furthermore, it would be an error to interpret infantile sexuality using adult concepts of sexuality: "The reflexes of lubrication and erection do not necessarily signify "interest" in sex. We cannot say what, if anything, infants' sexual reflexes "mean" to them" (Rathus, Nevid, and Fichner-Rathus, 2011, p. 401). As it regards the Oedipus complex: observations of pelvic thrusting do not sufficiently justify Freud's hypothesis that children are sexually possessive of their mothers or that they develop a hatred of their fathers based upon sexual jealousy, because sexual possessiveness and sexual jealousy are adult conceptions of sexuality and thus do not necessarily apply to infantile sexuality.

Bowlby (1969) writes that "probably in all mammals infantile sexuality is the rule", but he means to legitimate Freud; however, later in the same page, Bowlby (1969) also writes that "any observer of two- or three-year-old children playing together has noticed occasions when, with much excitement, a little boy and a little girl assume positions typical of adult coitus" (p. 158). Thus he presents us with a picture of infantile sexuality no longer confined to the Holy Trinity of psychoanalysis, to the fabricated love-triangle which has haunted the twentieth century, to theatre and to the myth of incest. Although Bowlby (1969) writes of a heterosexual encounter, homosexual encounters are often as frequent in little children, and they are not necessarily predictors of sexual preference later in life (the same could be said of heterosexual encounters in infants, they are not predictors of sexuality later in life). For instance, Cocteau (1923/2001), in his pseudo-autobiographical novel *Le Livre Blanc (The White Book)*, discusses how before puberty he and his schoolmates at an all-boys school engaged in sexual activities with each other, but as soon as they hit puberty his friends began frequenting female prostitutes in earnest and he was driven to conceal his own homosexuality, visiting female prostitutes, reluctantly, along with his friends, only to evade any suspicion of homosexuality.

Sexual curiosity often develops in children as early as 12 to 15 months of age, when they begin to play "Doctor" and display curiosity about sexual anatomy, but in the United States, children do not typically engage in genital play with others until about two years of age (Rathus et al., 2011, pp. 401-402). Infantile sexuality is a universal phenomenon; Spiro reports playful sexual activity between two two-year olds in an Israeli kibbutz:

"Ofer [a boy] and Pnina [a girl] sit side by side on chamber pots...Ofer puts his foot on Pnina's foot, she then does the same—this happens several times...Finally, Pnina shifts her pot away, then moves back, then away...they laugh...Pnina stands up, lies on the table on her stomach,...Ofer pats her buttocks...Ofer kicks Pnina gently, and they laugh...Pnina touches and caresses Ofer's leg with her foot [and] says "more more"...Ofer stands, then Pnina stands, both bounce up and down...both children are excited, bounce, laugh together...Pnina grabs Ofer's penis, and he pushes her away...she repeats, he pushes her away, and turns around...Pnina touches his buttocks." (Spiro, 1965, p. 225; as quoted in Rathus et al., 2011, p. 402)

At age two, when these two children should, according to Freud, be focused on their respective anuses as erogenous zones, or being "narcissistic" by masturbating, they are instead playing with each other in a sexual way ("more more") utilizing a wide array of body parts (buttocks, feet, legs), even the genitals. Even at an early age children interest themselves in the existence of others, and sometimes this interest is sexual.

Clearly, the real psychosexual development of human beings does not take place in the manner described by Freud: there is no oral stage, no anal stage, no phallic (Oedipal) stage, no latent stage, no genital stage. Psychoanalysis familializes sexuality—it reduces the sexual act to a familial ritual and the sexual relation to a family relation. By contrast, infantile sexuality, and by implication adult sexuality, is primarily social, involving the existence of others. This means that both infantile and adult sexuality are social, that sexual acts and sexual relations are also social rituals and social relations. (We do not oppose the social to the biological, we mean to oppose the social to the familial; of course, sexuality is also primarily biological, and sexual attraction is involuntary).

Thus we must agree with Deleuze and Guattari (1972/1977) that:

"The small child lives with his family around the clock; but within the bosom of this family, and from the very first days of his life, he immediately begins having an amazing nonfamilial experience that psychoanalysis has completely failed to take into account." (p. 47)

But we add that the child is not watched over by the family around the clock, that the child escapes from the bosom of the family, and that the child engages in social relations, sexual and non-sexual, in the secrecy of his or her own private life. The child has an inner world of its own which escapes the family, although the child may not escape the sociocultural milieu into which he or she is indoctrinated.

Sexual Imprinting in Birds Versus Sexual Plasticity in Humans

Konrad Lorenz published his book *Der Kumpan in der Umwelt des Vogels (The Companion in the Environment of Birds)*, in which he presents his theory of imprinting in birds, in 1935, and Freud published his work *Three Essays On the Theory of Sexuality* in 1905. It has been approximately a hundred years since these two men have presented their theories—one, imprinting, based on verifiable evidence, and the other, Freud's theories on sexuality, wildly speculative. It has been approximately a hundred years, and it has neither been proven that Freud is correct nor that imprinting occurs in humans. In fact, much evidence, of which we have presented only fragments, exists that Freud was fundamentally wrong about sexuality. Despite the lack of evidence for sexual imprinting in humans, some researches have argued that it does occur; as we shall see, their arguments are not well-founded, and evidence exists to suggest that sexual imprinting does not occur in humans.

Vos (1994) found that male zebra finches sexually imprint on their mothers and that males are likelier to be aggressive towards other males (or females) which bear morphological similarities to their father (pp. 9-10). Although Vos (1994) concludes that "it is likely that the object for aggressive behaviour is also influenced by early experience", he does not make the rash conclusion that there has been an "aggression imprint", and indeed, such a conclusion would be unjustifiable, since "overt aggression was relatively scarce, and observed in only 25 of the 57 males" (p. 9). Is this an example of the Oedipus complex and also of the Freudian concept of transference, wherein the individual transfers feelings for the parents at non-parental others? It is not likely. The zebra finches studied received biparental care (they were raised by both parents), and they did not exhibit sexual behaviors towards their own mothers or aggressive behaviors towards their own fathers, only to individuals *resembling* their mothers and sometimes to individuals *resembling* their fathers. A psychoanalyst may object that "repression" has occurred, but there is no way to empirically validate that "repression" has occurred. In addition, it is generally accepted that sexual imprinting "may be completed at a time when the appropriate reaction itself is not yet performed" (Immelmann, 1972, p. 151), i.e., sexual imprinting does not imply sexual desire for the mother, and the same can be inferred about the pseudo-Oedipal aggression observed (if indeed it was directed specifically at birds resembling the father and not just towards birds which looked like males, a point not clarified by Vos). These details which are at odds with Freud's hypotheses make it unjustifiable to describe zebra finches as "Oedipal birds"; regarding a scientific theory or hypothesis, the details are everything. Furthermore, as we shall see, avian sexuality is not equatable with human sexuality.

Even if one assumes, hypothetically, the existence of sexual imprinting in humans, the process of imprinting differs substantially from Freud's account of the Oedipus complex. In many avian species it has been demonstrated that during a critical (or sensitive) period in the infancy of the bird, the bird will learn, in the absence of any rewarding stimuli (for example, nourishment), to follow an individual (whether of its own species or not, whether animal or inanimate object) as its "mother", and later in life to mate with an entity which has traits similar to that of its "mother". Although a critical period for language acquisition has been established in humans, no critical period for acquisition of sexual preferences has been demonstrated. Moreover, in human subjects, a parent's traits are not necessarily a good indicator of which traits the subject finds sexually attractive.

Aronsson (2011), in her article "On Sexual Imprinting in Humans", which argues in favor of the existence of sexual imprinting in humans, writes that in heterosexual males, "a positive effect of mother was found on attraction to smoking, but not glasses, while a negative paternal effect was found on attraction to glasses, but not smoking" (p. 2). Smoking in the mother was correlated with the males finding smoking attractive, but the mother wearing glasses was correlated with the males not finding glasses attractive? This finding alone is at odds with sexual imprinting studies in birds, in which birds may imprint inanimate objects, such as ping pong balls, or other species (including humans). Sexual imprinting is absolute, deterministic, and rigid. On the other hand, Aronsson's (2011) finding regarding smoking and glasses is neither deterministic nor rigid; if sexual imprinting existed in humans, one would not find the variability that Aronsson (2011) found.

Aronsson (2011) goes on to state that "However, when maternal and paternal effects were investigated for a large number of artificial and natural traits, including smoking and glasses, an overall positive effect of opposite sex parent emerged in both heterosexual males and females" (p. 2). Aronsson (2011) seems to conceive of sexual imprinting as a statistical phenomenon—as something which can be inferred based on an "overall outcome" once statistical calculations are performed upon *correlation studies* involving a sample of individuals. However, sexual imprinting—especially in avian species in which it has been definitively demonstrated—is not a statistical phenomenon, it is a deterministic one. In avian species, there is no question of the traits of the imprinted object "balancing out" to an overall positive effect in a given sample—in each case, the bird reliably imprints upon the object presented to it during its sensitive period.

Furthermore, Aronsson (2011) hand-waves away sociological factors in explaining individuals' sexual preferences:

"For instance, children of smokers might be more likely to become smokers themselves, either because of social or because of genetic inheritance of the behaviour. Being a smoker, or growing up in a community where smoking is common, might potentially be associated with having a smoking partner. Note, however, that our main question neither was whether subjects inherit parents' behaviour, nor whether parents influence subjects' actual mate choice. What we investigate was subjects' sexual attraction to the investigated traits… Moreover, we could not find any associations in our data between parental and own smoking habits, or parental and partner's smoking habit...although it is possible that such associations exist. But even though this might explain that children of smokers mate with smokers (if they do), it does not explain the sexual preference for smoking. The preference must somehow have been acquired socially [sic]. Sexual imprinting provides a plausible mechanistic explanation for this acquisition." (p. 24)

Let us put aside the phrase "genetic inheritance of the behaviour", giving Aronsson the benefit of the doubt as meaning "genetic inheritance of predispositions likely leading to the behaviour", and examine her other claims. Although Aronsson

90

(2011) acknowledges that having a smoker as a parent would influence one becoming a smoker one's self, and thus in keeping the company of smokers, she goes on to state that she did not find any associations in her data between parental and one's own smoking habits, "although it is possible that such associations exist". She did not find any such association not because she surveyed for it and found no correlation, but because she did not survey for it to begin with. In fact, it has been demonstrated that the more exposure a child has to a parent smoking, the likelier the child is to smoke (Mays et al., 2014).

Thus, there is a confounding variable in Aronsson's (2011) study: whether or not the subject is a smoker. Based on the research of Mays et al. (2014) and others (Hill et al., 2005; Mahabee-Gittens et al., 2012; Gilman et al., 2009; Kandel et al., 2015), it is safe to say that one's parent being a smoker is a critical factor in whether or not one becomes a smoker. Thus, there are five different but related additional confounding variables which play major roles in the likelihood of a smoker being attracted to another smoker: classical conditioning (the association of smoking with pleasure, and thus the association of one who smokes with the pleasure of smoking), similarity (the tendency of people to like others who are similar to themselves), proximity (the tendency of people to like others who are near them), the mere exposure effect (the more a person is exposed to a stimulus, the more positively they evaluate that stimulus), and chemical addiction. (For references regarding similarity, proximity, and the mere exposure effect, see Kassin et al., 2014, pp. 346-348).

By including "chemical addiction" as a variable, we mean that regular smokers become addicted to the nicotine in tobacco products; addiction to nicotine is physio-chemical, it does not have anything to do with breastfeeding or bottle-feeding (orality), and the child may have become addicted to the substance by secondhand smoke from their parents; addicts of the same substance are likely to spend more time around each other, especially if they can absorb the substance through secondhand smoke from each other, therefore smokers are likelier to find each other attractive and mate with each other on the basis of their mutual chemical addiction.

These additional factors not only explain why a child of a smoker may mate with a smoker, but also why a child of a smoker may have a sexual preference for smokers. The preference was indeed acquired socially, and we have given a few reasons as to how that preference was acquired socially. The hypothesis of sexual imprinting in this case, however, is not "social" in its nature, but biological (a "critical period"), and is not reasonably demonstrated, especially when the confounding variables are considered.

The most grievous error of Aronsson's (2011) study is the confusion of correlation with causation. It is a well-known fact that correlation does not necessarily imply causation. Aronsson (2011), however, is inferring causation (sexual imprinting) from a correlational study, thus defying the laws of mathematics, logic and nature. Reliance on correlational studies and the illegitimate inference of causation from correlation occur near universally in studies which purport to prove or support the occurrence of sexual imprinting in humans.

In 2009, Bereczkei, Hegedus, and Hajnal published a paper which concluded that "Our results support the sexual imprinting hypothesis which states that children shape a mental template of their opposite-sex parents and search for a partner who resembles that perceptual schema", although their study relied on correlations. However, the behavioral ecologist Markus Rantala noticed that their reported correlations were unusually strong, and upon closer examination, the journal which published the study (*The Proceedings of the Royal Society B*) concluded that there were severe mathematical errors in the calculations of Bereczkei et al., leading to the retraction of the paper (Borrell, 2009). Although Bereczkei et al. claimed their errors were accidental, Rantala judged that "It seems that the authors have fabricated data to support a Freudian view of psychology, because there is no other evidence to support it" (as quoted in Borrell, 2009). As Borrell (2009) might say, Oedipus was wrecked. According to Borrell (2009), evolutionary psychologist Lynda Boothroyd takes the view that there is some evidence to support the Freudian hypothesis of mate selection in humans. In a 2007 study by Wiszewska, Pawlowski, & Boothroyd, it was reported that there was some correlation between the strength of a sample of females' relationships with their fathers and similarities in facial measurements between their fathers' faces and faces the women found attractive—however, the correlations were only between 20 and 40 percent (Borrell, 2009). Thus it appears that the evidence in support of sexual imprinting in humans is scant, if not non-existent, and reliant upon confusing correlation with causation.

Moreover, human sexuality is fundamentally different from avian sexuality: birds have fixed breeding seasons in which they go into heat and copulate, whereas every season is breeding season for humans (humans are always in heat, we have sex for pleasure, not because a biological clock dictates that we do). From an evolutionary viewpoint, sexual imprinting is an efficient mechanism for facilitating mate choice in avian species because it allows the bird to make a rapid mate choice under the time constraint of the breeding season. By contrast, sexual imprinting would serve no evolutionary advantage to humans, since humans are not under the time constraint of a breeding season, and thus are under no biological necessity to make a rapid mate choice. In fact, sexual imprinting would leave humans with an evolutionary disadvantage, since it would limit our mate selection to a single individual or a single "type" for our entire lives, thus wasting time—a breeding season which spans a lifetime—in which we could breed with other, perhaps fitter individuals. To illustrate more vividly the difference between avian breeding seasons and the human breeding lifetime, let us consider more concretely the difference in circumstances:

"Pair-forming colonial birds, for example, migrate to the breeding grounds where the nest sites will be established. Young and previously unmated birds, flying in as adults for the first time, must, like all other birds, establish territories and form breeding pairs. This is done without much delay, soon after arrival. The young birds will select mates on the basis of their sexual signals. Their response to these signals will be inborn. Having courted a mate they will then limit their sexual advances to that particular individual. This is achieved by a process of sexual imprinting. As the pair-forming courtship proceeds, the instinctive sexual clues (which all members of each sex of each species will have in common) have to become linked with certain unique individual recognition characters. Only in this way can the imprinting process narrow down the sexual responsiveness of each bird to its mate. All this has to be done quickly, because the breeding season is limited. If, at the start of this stage, all members of one sex were experimentally removed from the colony, a large number of homosexual pair-bonds might become established, as the birds desperately tried to find the nearest thing to a correct mate that was available. In our own species the process is much slower: We do not have to work against the deadline of a brief breeding season. This gives us time to scout around and 'play the field'." (Morris, 1967/2005, p. 65)

We do not struggle to find the nearest thing to a mate under the time constraint of a breeding season. Whereas avian mate selection is time-efficient and clear-cut due to sexual imprinting, human mate selection includes far more uncertainty and it is able to harbour such uncertainty because the time-frame in which human mating occurs is relatively vast. Human sexuality involves experimentation, a concept which defies the hypothesis of imprinting in humans. Humans often do not know what they want in a partner both socially and sexually, and often revise their mental model of their "ideal type" over time. Such experimentation would be disastrous and perhaps impossible if human sexual activity was limited to a breeding season. It is this variability in human sexual activity, its capacity to change over time, and the essentially experimental nature of human sexuality which leads us to describe it as *plastic*, and sexual plasticity likely has much to do with brain plasticity since the life of the psyche is the life of the brain. The definition of brain plasticity applies equally well to sexual plasticity: "Plasticity in the nervous system means an alteration in structure or function brought about by development, experience, or injury" (Gregory, 1987, p. 623; as quoted in Malabou, 2004/2008, p. 5). Sexual plasticity is dependent upon, and occurs through, brain plasticity.

Four Dimensions of Sexual Plasticity

To be more specific, there are four dimensions of sexual plasticity: sexual orientation, mate "choice", culture, and intra-individual development.

We recognize that innate preferences for a certain gender or both genders exist, but within that limit, there is significant variation in intra-individual sexual preferences. Moreover, the matter of sexual orientation is not as straightforward and rigid as pop culture and 20th and early 21st century folk psychology makes it seem. Consider, for example, the following phenomena:

"Many heterosexual people have had sexual experiences with people of their own sex (Mosher et al., 2005; Savin-Williams, 2006)...Gay males and lesbians, too, may engage in male-female sexual activity while maintaining a gay sexual orientation...Then, too, some people are bisexual but may not act on their attraction to members of their own sex (Edser & Shea, 2002)...Sexual orientation is not necessarily expressed in sexual behavior. Many people see themselves as gay or heterosexual long before they ever have sex with members of their own sex (Thompson & Morgan, 2008; Savin-Williams & Diamond, 2000)...People's erotic interests and fantasies may also shift over time. Gay males and lesbians may experience sporadic heteroerotic interests. Heterosexual people may have occasional homoerotic interests...Attraction to people of the other sex and people of one's own sex may therefore not always be mutually exclusive. People may have various degrees of sexual interest in, and sexual experience with, people of either sex (Hammack & Cohler, 2009; Thompson & Morgan, 2008)." (Rathus et al., 2011, p. 282)

In the industrial West, the recognition of the plastic nature of sexuality began with Alfred Kinsey (1948; 1953) and his groundbreaking research on sexuality. In the words of Kinsey and his colleagues:

"The world is not to be divided into sheep and goats...Only the human mind invents categories and tries to force facts into separated pigeonholes. The living world is a continuum in each and every one of its aspects." (1948, p. 639; as quoted in Rathus et al., 2011, p. 282)

Perhaps it is more accurate to say that the living world is dimensional in each and every one of its aspects. Kinsey and his colleagues (1948; 1953) conceptualized sexual orientation as a scale, or continuum, ranging from heterosexual to bisexual to homosexual. However, more recent research has challenged the notion of a continuum, and has conceptualized sexual orientation as dimensional, with heterosexuality and homosexuality constituting independent dimensions, which "allows for people to be as responsive to stimulation by people of the other sex as heterosexual people are, and as responsive to stimulation to people of their own sex as gay people are" (Rathus et al., 2011, p. 284). Some evidence has been found that "to some extent, women's sexual orientations are more flexible or plastic than men's, with women being somewhat more dependent on social experience" (Rathus et al., 2011, p. 282-285; Diamond, 2003; Thompson & Morgan, 2008; Bogaert, 2006; Storms, 1980; Lippa and Arad, 1997; Chivers and Bailey, 2005). In other words, in Western society, whereas men's sexual preferences tend to be bi-polar, or mutually exclusive (where the more sexually attracted a man is to a woman, the less he is to a man, and vice versa), women's sexual preferences tend to fit the dimensional model better. However, the inference that women's sexuality is inherently more plastic and dependent upon social experience than men's sexuality is an illegitimate inference. These studies were all performed in patriarchal, majority Christian Western societies in which there is rampant homophobia among males and a constant reinforcement of rigid gender roles—and in the gay community which has managed to arise in these Western societies, there is biphobia (hatred of bisexuals) due to the unfounded belief that claims to bisexuality are merely denials of being gay. The interiorization of social mores and roles—i.e., social experience—in males has likely had much to do with the finding that female sexuality is more plastic than male sexuality in Western society.

We repeat that many people have innate preferences for one or both genders in order to stress that innate preferences are not a matter of "free will", if it is possible for "free will" to exist. More precisely, one does not *choose* to prefer one gender over another or both genders. If one thinks that one can choose which gender one prefers it means that one is bisexual. Sexual desire is *involuntary*, and although we are conscious of what we desire, consciousness is not equatable with free will or intentionality; the factors which cause us to prefer one gender or both are unconscious, multi-fold, and not yet well-understood. The plasticity of sexual orientation, when it occurs, has as much to do with unconscious factors which affect sexual orientation "geologically", like tectonic plates beneath the earth, as it does with social experience. Sexual orientation cannot be changed by any known "therapeutic" means, and no credible psychologist or institution would claim that they are capable of changing it. There is evidence that genetic factors and levels of pre-natal hormones play a role in determining sexual orientation, but a definitive or universal biological cause has not yet been established (Rathus et al., 2011, pp. 291-293). The coexistence of the fact that sexual orientation cannot be changed by existing "therapeutic" means and the fact that sexual orientation can be plastic is supported by a large body of evidence, however difficult it may be to grasp theoretically. We stress that it is much more common to find examples of sexual plasticity *within* the limits of innate preferences, all the problems of defining sexual orientation considered.

Another dimension of sexual plasticity is mate "choice", or mate selection. Even when we drop the quotes typographically, we continue using "choice" in "mate choice" as if in quotes. We have put "choice" in quotes due to several reasons: a) it is as of yet unestablished whether or not "free will" is an empirical concept or to what extent it is a social construct, b) *we do not choose whom we desire, but are involuntarily attracted to them*, and c) even if we conceive of ourselves as making a conscious choice as to whom to desire, we are only rationalizing our involuntary feelings to ourselves a-posteriori.

All these problems considered, plasticity in mate choice does indeed occur. Due to the ethnocentric bias of Western psychology—especially the dominant views in "evolutionary psychology"—mate selection is considered from the point of view of monogamy as if monogamy in humans were human nature, a biological necessity, when in fact not all cultures hold sexual monogamy sacred nor practice it—if it is even possible to practice it in the strict sense of having only one sexual partner throughout one's entire life.

Monogamy is a myth, a social construct. It does not exist in nature, and in humans it must be constantly reinforced. To be more precise, *sexual monogamy* is a social construct (i.e., *fidelity* and *adultery* are social constructs), and scientists now use the term *social monogamy* to describe species in which a male and female form a pair-bond to rear young; social monogamy in no way implies sexual fidelity, and socially monogamous animals often indulge in sexual activities outside the pair-bond and have children by animals other than their "life-partner" (Reichard, 2003, pp. 3-5). Although these are well-established facts in ethology, they have gone largely ignored in psychology.

Other authors have made the case, quite convincingly, that human beings are by nature polygamous; we refer the interested reader to *The Myth of Monogamy* by Barash and Lipton (2001) and *Sex at Dawn* by Ryan and Jethá (2011). Even a merely casual glance at the kinship systems and sexual practices of other cultures definitively proves that, at the very least, human sexual behavior is dependent upon culture, and that humans are definitely not monogamous (neither sexually nor socially) by nature (Godelier, 2004/2012).

Mate choices of humans in Western psychology is often treated as if mate choice occurs only once in a human lifetime and that this single choice lasts an entire lifetime. Indeed, the hypothesis of imprinting in humans, which we have seen is inadequate, makes it so that there is only one possible mate choice for a given individual in their whole life. Bourdieu, in his book *Masculine Domination* (2001), calls the scientific legitimation of culturally relative social constructs the "eternalization of the arbitrary"; the sociological factors which make possible the deep-seated ethnocentric bias of Western psychology is not our immediate concern here, and we refer the interested reader to Bourdieu's book.

Whatever one may believe, it nonetheless *occurs* that a given individual is *involuntarily* attracted to *multiple* others. There is never *the One*. Human sexual desire always exists in a state of multiplicity. In this sense, we may say, along with Deleuze and Guattari (1972/1977) that sexual desire is always a multiplicity:

"It is only the category of multiplicity, used as a substantive and going beyond both the One and the many, beyond the predicative relation of the One and the many, that can account for desiring-production: desiring-production is pure multiplicity, that is to say, an affirmation that is irreducible to any sort of unity." (p. 42)

By the sexual plasticity of mate choice, we mean the multiplicity of sexual desire. The multiplicity of sexual desire allows one to account for the existence of both monogamous and polygamous human societies, and for the inevitable infidelities which occur in monogamous societies. As we have noted earlier, sexual desire and attachment are controlled by separate, independent brain mechanisms; attachment to a single individual does not affect the fact that involuntary attraction to others *occurs*, although it may or may affect the frequency of occurrence.

Another dimension of sexual plasticity is its cultural plasticity, the capacity of culture to shape sexuality. The cultural dimension of sexual plasticity is related to the concepts of *embodied cognition* (the functional equivalence of mind and body), evo-devo (ecology drives development), and the *enculturation of the brain* (the capacity of culture to alter structures in the brain). (For references on the enculturation of the brain, see: Lende and Downey, 2012). The mores, practices, and roles—i.e., the social constructs—of each culture regarding sex and sexuality become embodied in the brains and lives of its members; environment (i.e., culture) is inseparable from cognition and the body—and furthermore, the enculturation of the brain also means that the primary sex organ of the individual, the brain, is functionally shaped by culture.

As a single example of the cultural plasticity of sexuality, consider the following:

"Mangaians expressed concern when they learned that many Western women do not regularly experience orgasm. Orgasm is apparently universal among Mangaian women. Therefore, Mangaians could only assume that Western women suffered from some abnormality of the sex organs." (Rathus et al., 2014, p. 2)

But of course, the majority of Western women suffering from orgasmic disorder are not suffering because they have an abnormality in their sex organs, but because their brains and their bodies have been encultured by oppressive social constructs—or, phrased in another way, they embody the oppressive social constructs, the social constructs have been inscribed into their bodies, inscribed into their genitals.

Another dimension of sexual plasticity is intra-individual development. As we have already mentioned about infantile sexuality, infantile sexuality is not necessarily predictive of an individual's sexual preferences or behaviour later in life. Just like much else in human life, sexuality develops over the course of an individual's lifetime, and this is what we mean by the sexual plasticity of intra-individual development.

The evolutionary advantage of sexual plasticity is that it increases the number and variety of sexual partners, especially when contrasted with sexual imprinting, thus leading to increased chances of reproduction occurring and more variety in the gene pool when reproduction occurs. Increased variety in the gene pool as the evolutionary advantage of sexual plasticity is supported by and supports the Red Queen hypothesis of the evolution of sexual reproduction itself. "Red Queen" refers to an episode in *Through the Looking Glass* by Lewis Carroll in which Alice and the Red Queen run very fast for a very long time, only for Alice to realize that both of them have remained on the same chessboard on the same square under the same tree the entire time, moving almost no distance at all; the Red Queen explains that "it takes all the running you can do, to keep in the same place" (Carroll, 1896/1993, p. 179). Alice and the Red Queen run very fast for a very long time merely to keep in the same place—this is analogous to the biological function of sexual reproduction, which is an evolutionary arms race against pathogenic and parasitic organisms running near-infinitely through time, for generations and subsequently across vast stretches of geographic time, merely for organisms to exist. Leigh Van Valen proposed the Red Queen hypothesis in his paper "A New Evolutionary Law" (1973).

We have here presented a very brief sketch of sexual plasticity. A more comprehensive exploration of the concept of sexual plasticity is beyond the scope of the present work. The four dimensions of sexual plasticity and their relation to each other remains to be examined. Also, how sexual plasticity relates to brain plasticity remains to be worked out in detail. We refer the reader interested in brain plasticity and its philosophical implications to

Catherine Malabou's book *What Should We Do with Our Brains?* (2004/2008).

Malabou (2004/2008) writes that there are two dimensions of plasticity, the dimension of the "modifiable, formable, and formative" (p. 5), and the dimension of *plastique*, of plastic explosive:

"The word *plasticity* thus unfolds its meaning between sculptural molding and deflagration, which is to say explosion. From this perspective, to talk about the plasticity of the brain means to see in it not only the creator and receiver of form but also an agency of disobedience to every constituted form, a refusal to submit to a model." (p. 6)

We *burn* with passion. Sex is explosive—it explodes in orgasm, and it explodes limits. The limits society imposes, the limits we set ourselves. The plasticity of sexuality is what gives sex the potential to be a threat to all constituted forms, to the formal, and to the formative. The plasticity of sexuality opens the possibility for sex to be an act of revolution.

The Mnemonics of Pain: The Theory of Impression

Events associated with negative emotions, especially traumatic events, are *impressed* upon the mind, like a stamp or a red-hot brand. This theory of *impression* is supported by a large body of evidence.

The hippocampus, responsible for the encoding of memories, especially episodic memories, is anatomically intimate with the amygdala, which is responsible for the processing of emotional stimuli. So, at the physiological level, emotion and memory are inextricably linked.

Furthermore, negative emotions are likelier to lead to stronger memories of the salient stimuli than positive emotions, and the existence of a mechanism for this phenomenon makes sense from the perspective of natural selection:

"Although emotional memories are susceptible to distortion, negative emotion conveys focal benefits on memory for detail. These benefits make sense within an evolutionary framework. Because a primary function of emotion is to guide action and to plan for similar future occurrences (Lazarus, 1991), it is logical that attention would be focused on potentially threatening information and that memory mechanisms would ensure that details predictive of an event's affective relevance would be encoded precisely." (Kensinger, 2007, p. 217)

In order to survive, an organism needs to remember negative events in order to avoid or confront similar events in the future. Memory, even or especially the memory of the negative or traumatic, however painful it may be for the subject, is an adaptive mechanism of the brain. In the modern context of "functioning in society" (in quotation marks because "functioning", "society", and the value of "functioning" in "society" are questionable concepts), such a response may be construed as "maladaptive", which is a wholly subjective interpretation of dysfunctionality. In other words, although the "on edge" type of symptoms characteristic of PTSD are construed by psychiatrists as maladaptive (from the point of view of "adapting" to "society"), such responses are in fact adaptive to a given environment (war, gang violence, torture, rape culture).

The close proximity of the amygdala and the hippocampus means not only that emotionally salient events are likelier to be remembered, but also that strong emotional responses are likelier to facilitate the remembrance of memories which are associated with the aforesaid emotional responses.

Research reviewed by Buchanan (2007) suggests that:

"...the amygdala, in combination with the hippocampus and prefrontal cortex, plays an important role in the retrieval of memories for emotional events. The neural regions necessary for online [conscious] emotional processing also influence emotional memory retrieval, perhaps through the reexperience of emotion during the retrieval process."

The prefrontal cortex, which we have mentioned previously, in relation to Damasio's (1994) research, is highly important in the processing of emotional stimuli. Buchanan's (2007) review supports Damasio's (1994) claim that the prefrontal cortex is involved in the processing of emotional stimuli, and conversely, Damasio's research supports Buchanan's claim that the prefrontal cortex is important for memory retrieval.

There is evidence that emotionally salient stimuli are remembered at the expense of forgetting emotionally neutral stimuli (Brewin et al, 2007, pp. 455-457).

Emotional events trigger stress hormones which make more glucose (fuel for activity) available to the brain, signaling the occurrence of salient stimuli and stimulating the amygdala to initiate the formation of memory traces of the salient stimuli (Myers, 2014, p. 283). Repression does not occur. In other words, *traugmatic events cause us to remember information relevant to the traumatic stimuli much more strongly and vividly. When an event has emotional valence, especially when negative, it is remembered with vividness, it is impressed upon the brain.*

Freud conceives of repression as a dynamic force: "From this ego proceed the repressions, too, by means of which it is sought to exclude certain trends in the mind not merely from consciousness but also from other forms of effectiveness and activity" (Freud, 1923/1960, p. 7). Repression (and by extension resistance), proceeds from the ego—since the ego is a social construct, it necessarily follows that repression and resistance are social constructs because they depend upon the ego in order to exist. This elementary feat of reasoning is indeed supported by a large body of evidence.

Contrary to the popular view that traumatic events induce repression of memories of the trauma, traumatic events in fact enhance memories of the trauma and salient stimuli associated with the trauma; this fact is apparent to anyone who has actually experienced a traumatic event, but the Western institution of psychiatry has been slow to catch up due to its ideological limitations. It is only fairly recently, within the last few decades, that the Freudian myth of repression (which is not really original to Freud, but has been popularized by him) has been *begun* to be overturned. To clarify, the facts exist which refute Freud's hypotheses on repression, but popular acceptance of the facts has not yet occurred as of the beginning of the twenty first century.

Kihlstrom's (2006) *Trauma and Memory Revisited* provides a much more detailed review of the literature regarding trauma and memory than we have attempted here. In fact, we have done little more than recapitulate a few studies published since Kihlstrom's (2006) article which corroborate points he has already made.

Kihlstrom (2006) brings to awareness that repression, as it is discussed in psychoanalysis, needs to have been made entirely unconscious in order to function as described in psychoanalytic literature:

"There is a further question about the relationship between repression (or dissociation, for that matter) and suppression or denial. It is one thing to deny that something happened, or to deliberately avoid thinking about something that did happen, and another thing entirely to be unaware of something that happened— or, for that matter, to be unaware that one is avoiding thinking about something that happened...as both Sigmund and Anna Freud surely understood—the concept of repression, and the technique of psychoanalysis, only make sense if repression is deployed *un*consciously." (p. 266)

Freud (1923/1960) writes that his concept of the unconscious is obtained from the theory of repression (pp. 4-5). The repressed stands in opposition to the ego (consciousness), and the ego's *resistance* is a resistance "against concerning itself with the repressed" (Freud, 1923/1960, p. 7). In other words, the repressed is completely cut off from consciousness, it is "deployed" wholly unconsciously. Thus, Freud's concept of repression entails the ego being entirely unware of repression and the contents of repression, the repressed; the ego is "unaware that one is avoiding thinking about something that happened". Therefore, Kihlstrom (2006) is well justified in claiming that repression is altogether different from denial or directed forgetting, for the latter two processes do not entail amnesia of trauma (the repressed), whereas the concept of repression *is* dependent upon amnesia of trauma. Repression is not equatable with the subject pretending that nothing is wrong, nor with the subject pretending that a solution has been found to a problem when no such solution has truly been found; these latter two phenomena are akin to denial or directed forgetting, in which case the explicit memory of the existence of a problem would persist. Repression, on the other hand, means that the memory of a problem would itself be inaccessible to consciousness, and that one would not even be aware of this inaccessibility.

Kihlstrom (2006) concludes that repression is "a will-o'-the-wisp, a myth, an urban legend":

"The trauma-memory [amnesia of trauma] argument and recovered-memory therapy have been with us for more than 100 years, and have embedded themselves deeply into both our professional practices and our wider culture. But there was never any good evidence for either, and there still is none...nothing in the case literature justifies assertions that trauma impairs memory as a matter of course, or in the majority of cases or often—even *sometimes* seems too extreme. In view of the paucity of evidence that trauma causes amnesia, discussion of implicit memories of trauma seems pointless. Laboratory analogs of traumatic amnesia are models in search of a phenomenon; theories of traumatic amnesia are explanations in search of facts." (pp. 282-283)

Freud's hypothesis of repression fails to account for the fact that survivors of trauma remember the traumatic event quite clearly. People who suffer from PTSD experience unwanted flashbacks of traumatic events, often even nightmares directly concerning the events themselves; there is nothing in psychoanalytic literature to account for the simple fact of impression. Survivors of extreme violence—rape, torture, war, genocide—are haunted by memories of traumatic events. Trauma induces high levels of stress, releasing associated stress hormones which enhance memory (Myers, 2014, p. 431). There exist extensive volumes of art by the survivors of the atomic bombings of Hiroshima and Nagasaki, the Holocaust, and other tragedies personal and publicized, which deal directly with these tragic events; these artists wish to, among other things, impress the memories of these events into the minds of others so that similar events do not recur.

Freud has many misconceptions about PTSD, and handwaves away the problem it poses for his theories. After WWI, some attention was brought to the condition now known as PTSD—in Freud's time, it was called "traumatic neurosis" or "war neurosis". Freud erroneously compares PTSD to receiving concussions; but his distinction between concussions and PTSD, although the two sometimes overlap, we shall retain here (1920/1961, p. 10). It must be made clear that we are discussing patients without brain lesions who suffer from PTSD.

Freud acknowledged that in the dreams of PTSD patients, they relive the traumatic incident, that in a sense the patient is "fixated to his trauma", and compares it to a condition which was then called hysteria: like hysterics, we are told that survivors of trauma "suffer mainly from reminiscences" (Freud, 1920/1961, pp. 11-12). However, Freud ignores the obvious fact of impression and instead opts to attempt to fit the facts into his theoretical model:

"I am not aware, however, that patients suffering from traumatic neurosis are much occupied in their waking lives with memories of their accident. Perhaps they are more concerned with *not* thinking of it. Anyone who accepts it as something self-evident that their dreams should put them back at night into the situation that caused them to fall ill has misunderstood the nature of dreams. It would be more in harmony with their nature if they showed the patient pictures from his healthy past or of the cure for which he hopes. *If we are not to be shaken in our **belief** in the wish-fulfilling tenor of dreams by the dreams of traumatic neurotics*, we still have one resource open to us: we may argue that the function of dream, like so much else, is upset in this condition and diverted from its purposes, or we may be driven to reflect on the mysterious masochistic trends of the ego." (Freud, 1920/1961, p. 12; the latter emphasis is my own, especially upon "belief")

It is incoherent to say that the function of dreams is somehow "diverted from its purposes" in the absence of any brain injuries, because then there is no mechanism by which this supposed major change in function would occur, a change which would be on par with a brain lesion. Freud's other suggestion is rather atrocious: the nightmares of PTSD patients are due to "the mysterious masochistic trends of the ego". Freud is suggesting that sufferers of trauma have nightmares as a way of fulfilling their wish to relive their trauma, just like a sexual masochist, deriving pleasure from their own sufferings; if such a suggestion were actually applied to therapy, all it could do is induce guilt and shame in the patient. It is not empathetic to patients to claim that the memories they *suffer* from is actually wish-fulfillment, when the very reason the patients are suffering is due to their "reminiscences". The masochist, it must be remembered, is not really suffering when seeking out pain, since it is that pain which the masochist knows will bring them pleasure. The nightmares of PTSD patients do not bring them pleasure, they bring only pain. Here we have yet more contradictions in Freud's model of the mind: it is contradictory to claim that a) patients without any lesions in their brains have the alleged function of dreams irrevocably altered, or b) that patients both "*suffer* (unequivocally) from reminiscences" and that they wish to relive the reminiscences which make them suffer.

PTSD patients are neither faking nor fantasizing, and many of them have continued to suffer for years after the traumatic events due to *consciousness of trauma*; the facts of their existence are only comprehensible if one acknowledges that *traumatic events are impressed upon the brain, impressed upon the unconscious.*

Freud's theory of castration, outlined in his essay "Dissolution of the Oedipus Complex" (1924), strains credulity with its sheer absurdity (in my resistant and arrogant opinion), thus making it, among the other leaps of faith which psychoanalysis requires, the most incredible and fantastic leap of faith. Freud's idea that the Oedipus complex is repressed and thereby "resolved" due to the child's fear of being castrated (in the little girl, castration also goes by the name of "penis envy", but penis envy is still castration in the sense that it introduces a *lack*), relies upon his theory of repression. The fear of being castrated, or the disappointment of lacking a penis, both being two sides of castration, induces a powerful negative affect in the child, and due to this negative affect, the child represses the entire Oedipus complex, apparently destroying it if the repression is done right, but Oedipus is never fully destroyed because the analyst's hubris and paycheck depend upon the existence of Oedipus. Due to castration anxiety, infantile sexuality transitions from the Oedipus stage to the latency period. Freud's theory of castration cannot be true because if something such as castration anxiety actually occurred, it would be impressed into memory and haunt the child's life from infancy to adulthood. The reality of the impressionable nature of memory definitively disproves Freud's Oedipus complex, which Freud hypothesizes is typically repressed, especially when considered in conjunction with all the other reasons we have presented against it. We agree with Deleuze and Guattari (1972/1977) that the effect of Freud's concept of castration, either during analysis or through belief in his ideas, in a way of speaking castrates the unconscious, making it submissive to authority:

"Castration is at once the common lot—that is, prevalent and transcendent Phallus, and the exclusive distribution that presents itself in girls as desire for the penis, and in boys as fear of losing it or refusal of a passive attitude. This something in common must lay the foundation for the exclusive use of the disjunctions of the unconscious—and teach us resignation. Resignation to Oedipus, to castration: for girls, renunciation of their desire for the penis; for boys, renunciation of male protest—in short, "assumption of one's sex." This something in common, the great Phallus, the Lack with two nonsuperimposable sides, is purely mythical; it is like the One in negative theology, it introduces lack into desire and causes exclusive series to emanate, to which it attributes a goal, an origin, and a path of resignation...The Women's Liberation movements are correct in saying: We are not castrated, so you get fucked." (Deleuze and Guattari, 1972/1977, pp. 59-61)

As an operation upon the unconscious, castration is older than psychoanalysis, and it has persisted in culture. Even in science, where the dominant voices in Western evolutionary psychology, by telling just-so stories, attempt regularly to castrate the unconscious, to make one "assume one's sex" and be resigned to the way things are. Pharmaceuticals too are ways of castrating the unconscious, of inducing submissiveness and resignation. Psychoanalysis is only able to inject its metaphysics into the mind and castrate the unconscious through the social construct of repression; without repression, there is no basis whatsoever—even less than there already was—for the just-so stories of psychoanalysis.

We have relied here on Kihlstrom (2006), who provides a much more detailed deconstruction of Freud's concept of repression and a much more comprehensive body of evidence which refutes Freud's theory of repression. Not just laboratory analogs, but from the beginning the theories of psychoanalysis (the particulars covered in this section being what Kihlstrom calls the "trauma-memory argument", more properly described as the "amnesia of trauma argument", or simply "Freud's theory of repression", and "recovered-trauma therapy") have been bad science: "explanations in search of facts".

As we have mentioned earlier and have not ceased to mention, and as Kihlstrom (2006) writes, "emotional involvement makes events *more* memorable, not less" (p. 269), and this holds true for traumatic events as well as non-traumatic negative events, i.e., it is true for both trauma and everyday experience, and it is in light of these facts that we present the concept of *impression*. To understand the impressionable nature of memory, we only need to open our ears to those who spend their hours contemplating pain.

To illustrate our concept of impression, we conclude with an observation of Nietzsche, who knew the truth of memory far before physiology caught up with him:

"'Something must be burned in so as to remain in his memory; only that which never stops *hurting* will remain in his memory.' This is a principle of the oldest (unfortunately also the most enduring) psychology in the world. It might even be said that wherever solemnity, mysterious rituals and sombre hues are found in the lives of the men of the nations of the world, there is still some *active* remnant of that horror which once invariably accompanied all promises, pledges, and obligations. The past, the cruel, hard past, breathes in us and rears up in us again, when we become 'solemn'. Blood, torment and sacrifice were necessary for man to create memory in himself; the most dreadful sacrifices and forfeitures (among them the sacrifice of the first-born), the most loathsome mutilations (for instance, castration), the cruellest rituals of all the religious cults (for all religions are in essence nothing but systematic cruelty)—all these things originate from that instinct which found its most potent mnemonic to be the infliction of pain." (Nietzsche, 1887/2013, pp. 46-47)

Miscommunication: The Analyst's Failure to Listen

By supporters of psychoanalysis, Freud is often painted as a great listener. After all, the talking cure consists in large part of the patient talking to the analyst, and the analyst listening to the patient. But listening does not consist solely in hearing words as sounds—listening is the art of interpretation, for, as it regards words and non-verbals, it is only through a sufficiently accurate interpretation of what the other says and does, the signs of the other, that we are able to empathize with the other. Taking into consideration the analyst's method of interpretation—what the analyst listens for—psychoanalysis can be judged ineffective interpretation, and by implication ineffective listening, based upon the standards of communication science.

The analyst listens for what he considers "the royal road to the unconscious"—dreams, fantasies, speech errors, anything that might "signal" "unconscious" events—that is, the analyst *selectively listens* for phenomena which interests him (the analyst), interpreting such phenomena as mystical gateways into an unconscious, an unconscious which is conceived of in terms that reveal it to be a metaphysical entity completely at odds with the actual unconscious. This type of ineffective listening is called *selective listening*: "Selective listeners respond only to the parts of your remarks that interest them, rejecting everything else" (Adler and Proctor, 2014, p. 224). The analyst assumes that psychoanalysis is absolute knowledge, and that the psychoanalytic method is the best method of interpretation for arriving at absolute knowledge of the subjective world. However, the patient may know more about their own condition than it is possible for the analyst to perceive, due to the analyst's beliefs. Moreover, the analyst will be prone to interpreting a patient's complaints about the ineffectiveness of therapy or hostility towards the analyst as "resistance" or "transference", thus effectively ignoring any legitimate complaints or hostility that the patient has—this is an example of a type of ineffective listening known as *insulated listening*:

"Insulated listeners are almost the opposite of their selective cousins just described. Instead of looking for specific information, these people avoid it. Whenever a topic arises that they'd rather not deal with, those who use insulated listening simply fail to hear or acknowledge it. You remind them about a problem, and they'll nod or answer you—and then promptly ignore or forget what you've just said." (Adler and Proctor, 2014, p. 225)

Through the concepts of resistance and transference, the analyst is insulated against having to acknowledge complaints, the possibility that psychoanalysis is ineffective, and the possibility that they, the analysts, are harming patients. Instead of considering the patient's statements and behaviour from the patient's perspective, the analyst imposes the psychoanalytic interpretation upon the patient, over time manipulating the patient into being submissive and interiorizing the analyst's interpretation, oedipalizing the patient. With the concepts of resistance and transference, the analyst asserts a *pathos of distance* between himself and the patient, thereby preventing him from truly listening to and empathizing with the patient.

Furthermore, the analyst fosters a negative communication climate, or emotional tone of the relationship, in the analytic situation. In communication science, a communication climate is "the emotional tone of a relationship", and "a climate doesn't involve specific activities as much as the way people feel about and treat each other as they carry out those activities" (Adler and Proctor, 2014, p. 312). Communication climates are determined "by the degree to which the people [involved] believe themselves to be *valued* by one another"[emphasis my own], and this perceived value is conceptualized by social scientists by the concepts *confirming communication* and *disconfirming communication*: "Social scientists use the term *confirming communication* to describe messages that convey valuing and *disconfirming communication* to describe those that show a lack of regard" (Adler and Proctor, 2014, pp. 312-313). Disconfirming communication, more precisely, "shows a lack of value for the other person, either by disregarding or ignoring some important part of that person's message" (Adler and Proctor, 2014, p. 313; for additional references, see: Seiberg, 1976; Seiberg and Larson, 1971).

The analyst's selective listening and insulated listening are disconfirming, and thus foster a negative communication climate, because they evince a lack of regard for the empirical existence of the patient. Moreover, since the analyst is using an unempirical and fundamentally inaccurate method of interpretation (psychoanalysis), the analyst's explanations of the patient's problems to the patient are likely to be *tangential*, irrelevant or only very loosely connected. This makes the analyst's explanations classifiable as a type of disconfirming communication called *tangential responses*: "Conversational "takeaways" are called tangential responses. Instead of ignoring the speaker's remarks completely, the other party uses them as a starting point for a shift to a different topic" (Adler and Proctor, 2014, p. 314). The topic which interests the analyst most is Oedipus, of which we are tired of hearing.

Ineffective listening and disconfirming messages can be damaging, even fatal, to people suffering from emotional or mental problems.

Perhaps this will be more apparent if we consider a depressed patient. A depressed patient, feeling completely isolated in the universe, may benefit emotionally from a sympathetic listener. Moreover, a depressed patient may have a *particular* problem, of which he or she is well *conscious of*, and of which he or she desires to speak. For these reasons, among others, an analyst's poor communication skills, inherent to his profession and training, may be brutal—the analyst's interests may seem trivial to a depressed patient, for whom the important issues differ considerably from the analyst's interests—and thus a depressed patient may feel alienated by the analyst, unable to speak about what is making them depressed, and even more alone than before "therapy". If the patient's case of depression is severe, the brutality of the analyst's failure to listen could be the tipping point which drives them to suicide.

From the point of view of communication science, we may also glean a more accurate insight into patients who are labelled "schizophrenic" on the basis of "incoherent" or "aggressive" speech and behaviour—their speech and behaviour may only be "incoherent" and "aggressive" from the point of view of the analyst. If the psychiatrist is bullying the patient, should the patient ask for more and turn the other cheek in eager expectation? Furthermore, there is no objective basis by which the analyst, or any psychiatrist for that matter, may establish "incoherence" of someone's speech and gestures. The patient may have legitimate reasons for being aggressive to the psychiatrist, and the alleged "incoherence" may be attributable to the psychiatrist's failure to comprehend the patient.

The Crushing of Resistance

Now that we have systematically debunked a few of the concepts which are central to psychoanalysis—their non-existence is determined not only by implication of their dependence on each other, but also when examined in themselves—we are free to examine in greater detail the "analytic situation", that is, how the analytic situation is conceived of by psychoanalysis. Since Freud's model of the mind is a social construction and does not accurately represent the real workings of the mind, it is not possible for psychoanalysis to legitimately treat real illnesses or real problems. Moreover, models of the mind which build upon Freudian concepts—we refer here specifically to the psychoanalysts who come after Freud, from Jung, Rank, Klein, Lacan, all the way to Solms and the neuropsychoanalysts—likewise cannot serve as legitimate treatments for real illnesses or real problems because there are serious problems with such foundational concepts as *ego, id, superego,* and *repression.*

The analytic situation consists of the analyst removing the patient's resistance:

"Now we find during analysis that, when we put certain tasks before the patient, he gets into difficulties; his associations fail when they should be coming near the repressed. *We then tell him that he is dominated by a resistance*; but he is quite unaware of the fact, and, even if he guesses from his unpleasurable feelings that a resistance is now at work in him, *he does not know what it is or how to describe it.*" (Freud, 1923/1960, p. 7; italics my own)

"The fact that in the technique of psychoanalysis a means has been found by which the opposing force can be removed and the ideas in question made conscious renders this theory irrefutable. The state in which the ideas existed before being made conscious is called by us *repression*, and we assert that the force which instituted the repression and maintains it is perceived as *resistance* during the work of analysis." (Freud, 1923/1960, p. 4; italics in original)

As we have demonstrated, Freud's theory of mind is far from irrefutable—it is indeed thoroughly refutable. The patient experiences something—a feeling, or a failure to free associate—and the analyst dictates to the patient the "meaning" or "truth" of the patient's experience. As it regards the objective truth of psychoanalysis, it does not matter whether the patient agrees with the analyst or not—the patient is merely mislabeling his or her emotions and other mental phenomena as the analyst commands, and people's beliefs do not necessarily have any claim to objective truth.

The hypotheses of psychoanalysis posit supernatural causes to explain psychic life—*super*-natural because they cannot be verified to exist in the natural world—and they are no more or less valid than any of the world's religions or cults which likewise invoke supernatural causes to explain mental life. As is often noted by its critics, psychoanalysis is a religion; psychoanalysts are no more or less legitimate than traditional healers, including witch-doctors and priests. The fact that analysts need to go to school to become analysts means nothing; clergy need to go to seminary school, and healers in tribes also need to be educated by their predecessors. Psychoanalysis, like religion, is not medicine. Just as epileptics cannot be cured with exorcisms, mental illness cannot be cured with psychoanalysis (to the extent that it is possible for mental illness to exist); and just like cure-by-exorcism, the "talking cure" may be more damaging than helpful.

Since there is no *repression* or *repressed*, there is no force which maintains them, no *resistance* in the strict Freudian sense. But, no doubt, the patient will display resistance in the broader, socio-political sense—resistance to the assertions of the analyst, resistance to the "cure" by which the analysand is oedipalized and made submissive. Thus, there is an apparent disjunction between *resistance* as the analyst conceives it and *resistance* as a fact of analysis. In other words, the nature of the resistance displayed by the patient has nothing to do with repression. The patient's resistance to the analyst is of a socio-political nature, and it is only a psychological phenomenon insofar as it is a socio-political one as well.

We reiterate that the psychoanalyst sees it as his duty to weaken and destroy the patient's resistance: "In analysis these trends which have been shut out stand in opposition to the ego, and the analysis is faced with the task of removing the resistances which the ego displays against concerning itself with the repressed" (Freud,

1923/1960, p. 7). Since there is no repressed, the resistance which the analyst is crushing is the patient's resistance to being oedipalized. The "repressed", when it is not fabricated by the analyst, is confabulated by the analysand (Kihlstrom 2006). The Oedipus complex is not endogenous to the human mind—the patient must be made to believe in Oedipus. The first task of the analyst is to convert the patient into Freud's religion.

The patient is interrogated about non-existent phenomena, of which the analyst strives to convince them does in fact exist. If the patient disagrees or has something anoedipal to say, the analyst interprets it as resistance to be overcome. Psychoanalysis is cultural indoctrination, not medical treatment. To remove resistance means to remove the patient's own will. By this process, the patient's own will is destroyed and replaced by the will of the analyst—this is the process of oedipalization. There is no evidence to suggest that "the analyst knows best", especially given the body of evidence which refutes the analyst's assumptions about human nature, culture, psychology, and science. Psychoanalysis is in effect torture.

The analytic situation, as Deleuze and Guattari (1972/1977) put it, "is no longer a question of suggestion, but of sheer terrorism...Say that it's Oedipus, or you'll get a slap in the face" (p. 45). The psychoanalyst screams: "Answer daddy-and-mommy when I speak to you!" (Deleuze and Guattari, 1972/1977, p. 45).

Psychoanalysts speak of *transference*, the patient transferring feelings for the mother or father onto the analyst, but this is merely because the analyst wishes to be in a position of power and because the analyst wishes to, from the beginning and whether or not the analyst is aware of it, reduce the patient's discourse to mother problems and father problems. Transference has no explanatory or predictive value. Hostility towards the analyst is interpreted by the analyst as transference, and positive feelings towards the analyst is also interpreted as transference—and everything in between is interpreted as transference. There is no objective way to distinguish what is transference and what is not because transference is not an objective concept, but a highly subjective one. Its lack of objective basis suggests that the concept of transference is ideological. By interpreting the patient's feelings, speech, and actions towards the analyst as transference, the analyst affirms to himself his power over the patient, and in the process of analysis this interpretation becomes a self-fulfilling prophecy due to the analyst consistently treating the patient as an inferior. By this method, the analyst dominates the patient; this process is probably catalyzed by the patient's perception of the analyst as a legitimate doctor and the patient's perception of himself as suffering from an illness.

There is no "transference" as such—there is no infantile erotic desire of the patient towards the analyst. If the patient, either positively or negatively, treats the analyst as an authority figure, it is because the analyst *is* an authority figure in the patient's and analyst's shared sociocultural milieu. The analyst is a "doctor" and the analysand is a "patient"—this relationship is a sociocultural one, a relationship which consists of the respective social roles of "doctor" and "patient". The concept of transference is used by the analyst to dominate the analysand by exploiting the doctor-patient relationship. The use of the concept of transference is an abuse of authority and it is medical malpractice. From a sociological perspective, the concept of transference is an example of the systematic oppression of the populace by the bourgeoisie. The institution of psychoanalysis is a bourgeois institution which fraudulently claims to treat and cure patients in order to exert control over them.

Psychoanalysts themselves may be wholly unaware of the sociopolitical nature of psychoanalysis because they are indoctrinated into believing that psychoanalysis is a legitimate, objective science of the mind, and they are not accustomed to viewing psychoanalysis as a sociocultural phenomenon, let alone examining its claims empirically. The doctrines and texts of psychoanalysis can be described as ideology because they present themselves in the guise of truth, even to its practitioners and theoreticians, when in fact it consists only of illusions which serve the sociopolitical function of oppressing the populace and maintaining the power of the bourgeoisie.

From a sociological perspective, Freud's use of the word "resistance" is a clear example of appropriation. In psychoanalysis, *resistance* is something negative, a force to be excised. Resistance, in the sociopolitical sense, means people fighting for their freedoms. This appropriation of terms can only benefit the bourgeoisie, for whom resistance is indeed something which ought to be crushed. "Repression", too, is appropriated by Freud. Whereas the sociopolitical concept of repression is clear—it refers to the oppression or suppression of freedoms—Freud either neutralizes or confuses the sociopolitical usage of "repression" by endowing the word with a new meaning and introducing this new meaning into academic and popular discourse. The appropriation of "repression" also only benefits the bourgeoisie; by ignoring the sociopolitical discourse of repression and instead focusing on a psychoanalytic discourse of repression, the populace and academics are led to conflating the two concepts of repression and introducing into sociopolitical discourse new confusions, made all the more disastrous by the fact that the psychoanalytic concept of repression has no objective basis, i.e., it does not exist in nature.

Psychoanalysis is repressive in the sociopolitical sense—it is oppressive, suppressive—its aim is to control the wills of its patients, to take away whatever freedoms they have, and confine them to the discourse of "daddy-mommy", ultimately the discourse of a bourgeois ideology.

We agree with Deleuze and Guattari (1972/1977) that the "schizophrenic", or "psychotic", because they are "incurable", because they are incapable of being oedipalized, embody the spirit of resistance and of revolution. As a last measure to oedipalize the schizo, psychiatry destroys the schizo's brain by surgical or chemical means, thereby destroying the schizo's humanity, destroying the schizo's will and imagination. We need an excess of dopaminergic desire, an excess of passions, for that is the only way we can have an excess of rationality, an excess of reality. To be free, we need to be psychotics, we need to be schizophrenics.

Life Is A Work In Progress

As Solms and Turnbull write, in Freud's texts, the German word *Trieb* and its derivatives are often mistranslated as "instinct", when in fact a *trieb* is a *drive* (Solms and Turnbull, 2002, p. 117; Solms, 2013, p. 8). Solms and Turnbull (2002) further identify the drives as the appetitive drives and the dopaminergic seeking system: "Freud used the German term *Trieb* where we say "drive", but his English translators preferred to use "instinct". Where Freud spoke of "libidinal drives", we nowadays use the term "appetitive drives". Appetitive drives activate the [seeking] system..." (p. 117). Therefore, we shall use the term "death drive" instead of "death instinct", for "death drive" is a more accurate translation of Freud's concept of *Todestrieb*. According to Freud, the drives can be classified into two classes: *Eros*, the life drive (more or less synonymous with the sex drive), and *Thanatos*, the death drive— moreover, the life drive and death drive are *fused* to each, with problems only arising in their relation if they are de-fused, or separated, from each other (Freud, 1923/1960, pp. 37-39).

Therefore, if the death drive existed, we would expect to find it, under ordinary circumstances, fused to the sex drive, or at the very least, to find it in the seeking system. However, we find no such thing. Solms and Turnbull (2002) describe the activity of the seeking system thusly:

"[The seeking] system is heavily activated during sexual arousal and other *appetitive* states...How is the [seeking] system normally activated? There is a range of *need-detector* mechanisms in the hypothalamus (particularly the lateral and ventromedial nuclei, with extensive connections to other brain regions). These detectors constantly "sample" the internal milieu to maintain its delicate economy. Different hypothalamic regions switch these detector systems on (they act like "accelerators") and off (acting like "brakes"). One of these systems, for example, regulates your core body temperature. It ensures that your temperature stays in the (very narrow) correct range. There is also a thirst detector, a hunger detector, even a "sexual-need" detector." (pp. 116-117)

There is need-detector for sexual-need, but there is no need-detector for a death-need. That is, there is no mechanism which checks to see if the body has sufficient levels of death within it. The drives all operate in the mesocortical-mesolimbic system—if no mechanism for a death drive is found in the mesocortical-mesolimbic system (especially considering Freud's claim that the death drive is fused to the sex drive), then there is no death drive. If a *Todestrieb*, or death drive, existed, we would expect to find a correlative need-detector mechanism in the hypothalamus (like with all the other appetitive drives), but no such mechanism exists, therefore we can conclude that there is no death drive.

Freud writes that evidence for the fusion of the life drive and the death drive can be found in the relationship of "love" and hate:

"For the opposition between the two classes of instincts we may put the polarity of love and hate. There is no difficulty in finding a representative of Eros; but we must be grateful that we can find a representative of the elusive death instinct in the instinct of destruction, to which hate points the way. Now, clinical observation shows not only that love is with unexpected regularity accompanied by hate (ambivalence), and not only that in human relationships hate is frequently a forerunner of love, but also that in a number of circumstances hate changes into love and love into hate. If this change is more than a mere succession in time—if, that is, one of them actually turns into the other—then clearly the ground is cut away from under a distinction so fundamental as that between erotic instincts and death instincts, one which presupposes physiological processes running in opposite directions." (Freud, 1923/1960, pp. 40-41)

We shall put aside the problematic usage of the word "love", which is a culturally relative social construct. Along the lines of a Freudian interpretation of "love", we infer that by "love" Freud means "sexual desire". According to Freud's drive theory, sexual desire can change into aggression ("hate") and is often accompanied by aggression because of the fusion of the sex drive and the death drive. Paradoxically, Freud also claims that this can occur from a de-fusion of the two classes of drives, and he gives sadism as an example of a de-fusion (Freud, 1923/1960, p. 39). The death drive,

Freud tells us, is the drive of aggression, in both humans and other organisms:

"It appears that, as a result of the combination of unicellular organisms into multicellular forms of life, the death instinct of the single cell can successfully be neutralized and the destructive impulses be diverted on to the external world through the instrumentality of a special organ. This special organ would seem to be the muscular apparatus; and the death instinct would thus seem to express itself—though probably only in part—as an instinct of destruction directed against the external world and other organisms." (Freud, 1923/1960, pp. 38-39)

Freud equates the aggression ("hate") of the frustrated lover with the "aggression" (the "drive of destruction") of animals (his description seems to apply most to predatory animals such as the tiger), and both phenomena are taken to be examples of the same physiological mechanism, the death drive. However, the aggression ("hate") of the frustrated lover is qualitatively and neurologically different than the "aggression" of predatory animals. The lover's love—whether considered sexually or emotionally—"changes" (more accurately, gives rise to) "hate" (aggression) because of the lover's unmet need (either sexual need or emotional need, or both). By contrast, the "aggression" of predatory animals is a natural biological drive and it is not driven primarily by a frustrated desire.

Solms and Turnbull (2002) write on aggression that:

"More than any other system, the RAGE (or "anger-rage") system is activated by states of *frustration*—when goal-directed actions are *thwarted*. The term "anger-rage" is used to denote the *feeling state* associated with the arousal of this system. This term is necessary because not all aggressive behavior is activated by the [rage] system. Neurobiologists distinguish between two (or three) different types of *aggression*. The [rage] system is associated with only one of them: so-called "hot" aggression. The "cold" type of aggression, associated mainly with predatory behavior, has little to do with feelings of anger or rage; rather, it has to do with appetitive *seeking* and is therefore driven by the dopaminergic system described above...The key structure in triggering anger-rage is the *medial* nucleus of the amygdaloid complex. This [rage] system courses through the bed nucleus of the stria terminalis and (anterior, ventromedial, and perifornical) hypothalamus before it, like all the other basic emotion command systems, projects down into the (dorsal) PAG." (pp. 123-125)

The cold aggression of predatory animals is controlled by a different brain mechanism than the rage-anger ("hate") experienced by the frustrated lover. Freud equivocates when he compares the two and assigns to them the same mechanism, the death drive. Love is not a death-wish; neither is aggression, for that matter. To employ the language of neurobiologists, cold aggression (of predatory animals) and hot aggression (such as that of frustrated lovers) are physiologically distinct. Predatory animals feel neither anger nor rage towards their prey. Predatory animals hunt their prey due to a *seeking* drive.

From the evidence of absence of the death drive, we can further conclude that Freud was wrong in his conjectures that sadism and epileptic seizures are caused by the de-fusion of the sex drive from the death drive. Sadism—more specifically, sexual sadism—operates through the seeking system, for it is a sexual desire, and although its causes are not fully known, we can definitively rule out Freud's hypothesis that it is representative of a death drive. As it is now widely known, epileptic seizures are caused by abnormal and excessive brain cell activity.

Hoffman (2004) illegitimately attempts to legitimate the death drive by interpreting apoptosis, programmed cell death, as the mechanism of the death drive. Hoffman (2004) even goes as far to say that Freud's theory of the death drive is supported by the work of thousands of cell biologists and molecular biologists:

"Freud's largely solitary, but prescient, musings that engendered *Beyond the Pleasure Principle* in 1920 [in which Freud first presented his theory of the death drive] compare favorably with the work produced by thousands of molecular and cell biologists during the ensuing years." (Hoffman, 2004, p. 68).

We have already demonstrated, using evidence from neurobiology, why the death drive is a social construct and not a scientific concept. Apoptosis is not an appetitive drive, nor does it have anything directly to do with the sex drive nor with any form of aggression, nor does apoptosis cause sadism, nor does it cause epileptic seizures. Therefore, apoptosis cannot be the mechanism of the death drive. Hoffman (2004) is at best making a weak analogy, and at worst fabricating an illusory connection. Both phrases "death drive" and "programmed cell death" have the word "death" in them, but that is about as far as the connection goes.

Hoffman's (2004) equivocation of apoptosis with the death drive is apparent as an equivocation to anyone who is willing to consult a neuroscience or biology textbook in order to discover what apoptosis actually means. Kalat (2016) offers the following description of apoptosis in his neuroscience textbook *Biological Psychology*:

"Initially, the sympathetic nervous system forms far more neurons than it needs. When one of its neurons forms a synapse onto a muscle, that muscle delivers a protein called nerve growth factor (NGF) that promotes the survival and growth of the axon (Levi-Montalcini, 1987). An axon that does not receive NGF degenerates, and its cell body dies. That is, each neuron starts life with a "suicide program": If its axon does not make contact with an appropriate postsynaptic cell by a certain age, the neuron kills itself through a process called apoptosis, a programmed mechanism of cell death. (Apoptosis is distinct from necrosis, which is death caused by an injury or a toxic substance.) NGF cancels the program for apoptosis; it is the postsynaptic cell's way of telling the incoming axon, "I'll be your partner. Don't kill yourself."

The sympathetic nervous system's way of overproducing neurons and then applying apoptosis enables the CNS to match the number of axons to the number of receiving cells. When the sympathetic nervous system begins sending axons toward the muscles and glands, it doesn't know the exact size of the muscles or glands. It makes more neurons than necessary and discards the excess. In fact, all areas of the developing nervous system make far more neurons than will survive into adulthood. Each brain area has a period of massive cell death, becoming littered with dead and dying cells. This loss of cells is a natural part of development. In fact, loss of cells in a particular brain area often indicates maturation. For example, teenagers lose cells in parts of the prefrontal cortex while neuronal activity increases in those areas (Sowell, Thompson, Holmes, Jernigan, & Toga, 1999). Maturation of successful cells is linked to simultaneous loss of less successful ones." (Kalat, 2016, pp. 122-123)

Perhaps now it is more clear how apoptosis differs from the appetitive drives. The appetitive drives are functions of large numbers of neurons organized into functional systems. Apoptosis is the function of an individual cell (in our discussion, we are considering neurons, or nerve cells). Moreover, apoptosis does not entail the "neutralization" of cell death in order for the "destructive impulse" of the cell to be diverted onto the external world via the muscular apparatus, as Freud describes the activity of his death drive. Apoptosis in neurons does not move the organism towards its own death—on the contrary, apoptosis of individual cells "streamlines" the brain so that the organism is better equipped to survive. Freud predicts that overactivity of the death drive moves an organism towards its own death. On the other hand, if apoptosis does not occur—meaning that not enough cells are undergoing pre-programmed cell death—cells proliferate and become tumors, leading to cancer and death for the organism. Freud's death drive functions to move the organism as a whole to its own death. Apoptosis is a regulatory mechanism which "sacrifices" parts of the organism, individual cells, so that the organism as a whole may survive more efficiently and thereby live longer. The death drive is self-destructive. Apoptosis is a natural part of development, of the growth and maturation of an organism.

The death drive introduces a *telos* (purpose) into nature: "The aim of all life is death" (Freud, 1920, p. 38; as quoted in Hoffman, 2004, p. 65). In Freud's metapsychology, life has death as its purpose, and insofar as it introduces a telos into life, his metapsychology is theology and metaphysics. Freud makes death the first cause and final cause of life, the primordial state from which life began and towards which life strives to return: "All instincts tend towards a restoration of an earlier state of things" (Freud, 1920, p. 37; as quoted in Hoffman, 2004, p. 65). Freud makes it clear that he believes in the death drive for comfort, which, though he does not mention it, is the same reason why many people turn to religion:

"Perhaps we have adopted the belief because there is some comfort in it. If we are to die ourselves, and first to lose in death those who are dearest to us, it is easier to submit to a remorseless law of nature, to the sublime [Necessity], than to a chance which might perhaps have been escaped." (Freud, 1920/1961, p. 39)

The death drive is God, it guarantees that all deaths happen due to the Will of God, according His Divine Plan, His sublime Necessity. Of course, there is no "sublime Necessity" to death, it is indeed a chance which might perhaps have been escaped. For the same reason that evolution has no purpose, life has no purpose: time has neither an inherent meaning nor purpose. There is no telos in nature, neither for the species nor for the organism. It is on the basis of the inherent meaninglessness of nature that Darwin posited his theory of natural selection and that decades later biologists formulated the Modern Synthesis. The ideology of the death drive is the same as the ideology of the Will of God: by making death a "sublime Necessity", death is rendered harmless, something automatic which does not require any thought, and thereby life is also rendered as something automatic which does not require thought, and our pathos for those suffering diminishes because it is made the Will of God for them to suffer, as opposed to the reality of suffering, which is that all of it is due to a chance which might perhaps have been escaped.

That there is an element of chance to death implies that there is an element of chance to life. As Pindar and Sutton (2000) put it: "Life is a *work in progress*, with no goal in sight, only the tireless endeavour to explore new possibilities, to respond to the chance event - the singular point - that takes us off in a new direction" (Pindar and Sutton, 2000, p. 13; in Guattari, 2000; emphasis my own). Both the evolution of species and the life of an individual organism are works in progress, an experimentation and a resistance to death, and since it proceeds by chance as much as by the necessities of the laws of nature, life is fundamentally a gamble, and death is the losing hand.

Anthropology Versus Western Psychology

By deconstructing Freud's concepts of repression and the Oedipus complex at length, we have arrived at a means of critiquing the superego. The superego does not only mean one's inner sense of duty, what is called the "categorical imperative" by Kant, nor does it only mean one's ideal self. The superego, as it is conceived by Freud, is the ghosts of one's father an entire lineage of fathers forever occupying one's head, peremptorily giving orders and judging us for each of our actions, a homunculus in our heads which sprang into existence to keep us from fucking our mothers.

According to Freud,

"[The superego's] relation to the ego is not exhausted by the precept: 'You *ought to be* like this (like your father).' It also comprises the prohibition: 'You *may not be* like this (like your father)—that is, you may not do all that he does; some things are his prerogative.' This double aspect of the ego ideal [the superego] derives from the fact that the ego ideal had the task of repressing the Oedipus complex; indeed, it is to that revolutionary event that it owes its existence...The child's parents, and especially his father, were perceived as the obstacle to a realization of his Oedipus wishes; so his infantile ego fortified itself for the carrying out of the repression by erecting the same obstacle within itself. It borrowed strength to do this, so to speak, from the father, and this loan was an extraordinarily momentous act." (Freud, 1923/1960, p. 24)

We have several reasons for declaring that there is no superego: the non-existence of the Oedipus complex, the non-existence of repression, and the false dichotomy of reason and the passions. Children are able to learn concepts even before they learn how to speak (Havy and Waxman, 2016), therefore it is reasonable to believe that children are indoctrinated into their socio-cultural milieu before the age (years 3-6) when purportedly the Oedipus complex occurs and the superego forms. Parents definitely play a major role in indoctrinating children into society, but so does every other individual, and even inanimate objects, which the infant encounters. Indoctrination begins at birth. The roles fulfilled by the parents do not encompass all the other roles in society which the child will have to react to or enact. Simply put: society and culture and their morals and taboos are too complicated to be reduced to the Oedipus complex.

It is primarily society and culture which are responsible for the development of the child's ideal self and categorical imperatives. Parents do not exist "in themselves", they are the embodiments of a socio-cultural milieu. The roles "father" and "mother" only make sense when contrasted with other roles which are enacted by non-parental and non-familial others. Yes, there is a biological father and a biological mother, but these facts of biology do not determine, at least in humans, the social roles of "father" and "mother". In fact, a "father", as the term is understood in Western societies, is not necessary for child-rearing. In a society without the father role, the possibility of an Oedipus complex never arises, and discussing Oedipus within such a culture would be sheer nonsense. Freud's theory of the Oedipus complex is completely at odds with the kinship systems of the majority of non-Western civilizations, with only a handful of exceptions, such as the "phallo-narcissistic" Kabyle society studied by Pierre Bourdieu in his book *Masculine Domination* (2001).

Instead of teaching Freud to children in the psychology classroom, it would be infinitely more insightful for the students to learn about the findings of cultural anthropologists. By teaching Freud, psychology teachers indoctrinate their students into a culture, teach them to work from an ethnocentric bias, and obscure students' understanding of the mind. By teaching the findings of cultural anthropologists, psychology teachers could move their students' understanding of the mind beyond the confines of a particular culture, and provide students with facts about how people actually think across the globe.

Malinowski (1927/2001), in his book *Sex and Repression in Savage Society*, already provides plentiful evidence that the terms of the Oedipus complex do not apply to some other cultures. The culture he discusses at length is that of the Trobriand Islanders, in which the maternal uncle disciplines the child, not the father, and as a result, the child has an ambiguous relationship with his uncle and a more pleasant relationship with his father. Therefore, according to Malinowski (1927/2001), the child's ambiguous relationship to a parental figure has to do with *power*, not sexuality. Malinowski's

(1927/2001) findings are corroborated by the research of Straus, Douglas, and Medeiros (2014, p. 120), who demonstrate that corporal punishment weakens the parent-child bond; for the Trobriand islanders, the child-uncle bond is weakened by the maternal uncle's disciplinary actions.

In addition, let us briefly consider the Mosuo civilization—a matriarchal civilization in which women are the owners and inheritors of property. Mosuo children are traditionally raised in the mother's household and the biological father lives separately from the biological mother—in his own matrilineal household. The Mosuo could be described in Western terms as a "fatherless society", but this is an inadequate description because they do not *lack* fathers, there is no *absence* of the father—they have no fathers because there is no need for fathers, or more precisely, the father role—there are no fathers to begin with. In Mosuo society, this "fatherlessness"—a term which does not really apply, since there is no father role to begin with—does not inherently injure their children or their society (Stacey, 2009, p. 294). In fact, the children are fine.

Biology does not determine social bonds, and our contemporary taken-for-granted family relationships are socially constructed and culturally relative, not natural and universal (Stacey, 2009, p. 294).

We agree wholeheartedly with Margaret Mead's conclusions in her book *Coming of Age in Samoa* (1928/2001) that Western civilization has much to learn from other civilizations about healthy attitudes towards sexuality, gender relations, and biology. Mead (1928/2001) presents Samoan civilization as an ideal model. We suggest that, along with Samoan civilization, we should also consider Mosuo civilization as an ideal model, *mutatis mutandis* for homosexual as well as heterosexual sex life:

"Traditional Mosuo family values radically separate sexuality and romance from domesticity, parenting, caretaking, and economic bonds. Sex life is strictly voluntary and nocturnal, while family life is obligatory and diurnal. The cultural attitude toward heterosexual desire is permissive, relaxed, and nonmoralistic, so long as individuals observe strict verbal taboos against discussing their erotic activities among relatives or in mixed gender settings... Among the many extraordinary features of traditional Mosuo family and kinship, perhaps none is as rare as the equality and autonomy it afforded women over their sexual and procreative lives. Mutual desire alone governed romantic and sexual unions for women and men alike. Parents and kin did not meddle or concern themselves with the love lives of their daughters (or sons), because mate choice carried almost no implications for the family or society. Under the *tisese* system, men, who must "walk back and forth," exercise slightly more initiative (or bear somewhat more of a burden) than women when it comes to petitioning for sexual and romantic access. However, Mosuo women can freely refuse any undesired visits and explicitly invite desired ones. They do not suffer the nearly universal double standard that regulates women's sexuality elsewhere. Mosuo culture does not venerate female chastity or judge women's sexual behavior differently from men's. Girls and boys alike learn traditional courting songs and receive encouragement to desire, pursue, and enjoy (hetero)sexual lovers." (Stacey, 2009, pp. 290-292)

A Dream Within A Dream, Part I: The Ventromedial Prefrontal Cortex, Or, Emotional Learning as the Function of Dreams

"*All* that we see or seem
Is but a dream within a dream."
—Edgar Allan Poe, "A Dream Within A Dream"

In dreams, consciousness exists, but it is altered. Hobson (2002) describes dreaming consciousness as an "altered state of consciousness":

"Dreaming, then, is an altered state of consciousness...We delusionally believe that we are awake when we are in fact asleep; we delusionally believe that we are perceiving a real outside world, whereas we are actually creating that world without benefit of external stimuli; and we are not capable of critically observing, assessing, and appreciating our delusional and confabulatory awarenesses." (pp. 7-8)

What, however, is the nature of this delusion? We do not think we are awake when we dream because we choose to believe that we are awake; rather, we believe we are awake because we experience a world which appears to us—during the dream—as indistinguishable from the real world. It is only upon waking that we realize that the dream-world was in fact quite "bizarre" when compared to the world we experience when awake. This hints at two things, one of which is often remarked upon: in dream-consciousness, awareness is diminished when compared to waking consciousness. The other, not so often remarked, is that the brain is a dream-machine which produces dreams: the brain has a "reality-engine" with which it produces a virtual reality for our dream-consciousness to inhabit.

We call to attention once again Damasio's (1999) categorization of consciousness as "core consciousness" and "extended consciousness". As stated in a previous section, core consciousness is generated by the upper brainstem and extended consciousness by the cortex. Core consciousness is affective consciousness, and extended consciousness encompasses complex cognitive functions like abstract reasoning, working memory, episodic memories, and attention. Extended consciousness is dependent upon core consciousness, but core consciousness can exist in the absence of extended consciousness. In dreams and in waking life, the consciousness which persists is core consciousness, which is affective consciousness. The activity of extended consciousness, which is produced by the cortex, is diminished during sleep and dreams, thus accounting for dream-bizarreness.

This conceptual framework of the dreaming brain is corroborated by the fact that during REM sleep (during which most dreams, and the most vivid and emotional dreams, tend to occur), brainstem activity increases while cortical activity decreases: "During REM...both DLPFC [dorsolateral prefrontal cortex] and the locus coeruleus become less active. This presumably inhibits the ability of DLPFC to allocate attentional resources (and the dreaming brain classically pays little attention to bizarre incongruities in dreams)" (Stickgold et al., 2001, p. 1056). In addition, during REM sleep, the mesopontine tegmentum of the brainstem is active; cholinergic neurons in the mesopontine tegmentum trigger REM sleep (Solms, 2000, pp. 843-844).

However, it must be noted, as the title of Solms's (2000) neuroscientific paper states, "Dreaming and REM sleep are controlled by different brain mechanisms". Solms writes that "the principle that REM can occur in the absence of dreaming and dreaming in the absence of REM is no longer disputed" (Solms, 2000, p. 844). Between 43% and more than 50% of NREM awakenings report awareness of complex mentation during sleep, i.e., dreams; the average NREM dream is "thought-like", but approximately 10-30% of NREM dreams are indistinguishable from REM dreams (Hobson's more conservative estimate of this latter figure is 5-10%); in addition, approximately 5-30% of REM awakenings report an absence of dreams; (as reported in Solms, 2000, pp. 844-845).

Although reports on the correlation of dreaming and pontine brain stem lesions are lacking due to the fact that brainstem lesions which are too large obliterate consciousness altogether, a few cases have been reported in which dreaming is preserved in patients with pontine brainstem lesions (Solms, 2000, p. 845). In any case, the relative frequencies of the occurrence of dreams in NREM sleep stages and the relative absence of dreams during REM suggest that although REM sleep (and the cholinergic, pontine brainstem mechanism which produces REM sleep) facilitates vivid dreams, it is not the cause of dreaming.

A plethora of lesion studies points to two forebrain areas which are responsible for generating dreams: the parieto-temporo-occipital (PTO) junction located in the posterior forebrain, and the ventromedial prefrontal cortex (vmPFC) located in the anterior forebrain (Solms, 2000, pp. 846-848). Lesions to either of these two areas results in total or near-total loss of dreaming (depending on the extent of the lesion), and furthermore, the brainstem and REM sleep are completely intact and preserved in the cited lesion studies (for references concerning these lesion studies, see Solms, 2000, pp. 846-848).

Solms (2000) reports that the PTO junction is responsible for mental imagery, spatial cognition, and quasi-spatial symbolic operations, thus its function in dreaming is relatively obvious: the PTO junction is responsible for generating the images we perceive as the dream-world (pp. 846-848). De Benedictis et al. (2014) describe the PTO junction as "a complex brain territory heavily involved in several high-level neurological functions, such as language, visuo-spatial recognition, writing, reading, symbol processing, calculation, self-processing, working memory, musical memory, and face and object recognition" (p. 132), which is consistent with Solms's (2000) description of functions of the PTO junction and its role in dreaming. The PTO junction's importance in dreaming partially explains the hyper-associative nature of dreams so often noted by dream researchers. But why are associations so important to dreams? Why is the dream-world produced at all? To ask why the dream-world is produced at all is to ask why one dreams, i.e., to ask what is the function of dreaming. For an answer, we must turn to the other cortical region responsible for dreaming, equally as important as the PTO junction for dreaming, the vmPFC.

The vmPFC is part of the brain's dopamine circuit (Solms, 2000, pp. 846-847). The vmPFC is interconnected with the PAG (Price, 2007, p. 63), the location where core consciousness is produced, thus supporting our claim of the essentially affective nature of dreams. The majority of the evidence connecting the vmPFC and dreaming comes from prefrontal leukotomies performed upon "schizophrenic" patients in the hopes of "curing" them. (A note: We use "schizophrenia" and "psychosis" throughout this text as if in quotes, due to the lack of sufficient evidence that these socially constructed concepts actually correlate with a real disease that has a consistent, universal, and unequivocal biopathology). Lesioning the vmPFC did indeed end their hallucinations, if they had any, but it also extinguished their ability to dream—not to mention the damage it did to their imagination and their will:

"Damage along this [seeking] system produces disorders characterized by reduced interest, reduced initiative, reduced imagination, and reduced ability to plan ahead (Panksepp 1985). Lack of initiative or *adynamia* – where the patient does nothing unless instructed...was a commonly observed side effect of orbitomesial prefrontal leukotomy..." (Solms, 2000, p. 847)

Leukotomies and lobotomies are procedures of surgical oedipalization. Schizophrenia and psychosis are today treated by antipsychotics, "chemical leukotomies", which decrease activity in the dopamine circuit with chemicals which "inhibit excessive, unusually frequent, and vivid dreaming" and produce a "loss of interactive interest in the world" (Solms, 2000, p. 847)—chemical oedipalization. Leukotomies, whether surgical or chemical (as we find today), are an unethical procedure, procedures of oedipalization which transform the patient into a submissive "hospital creature". The dopamine circuit, in both its roles as seeking system and fear system, serves a vital function for the organism, and impairing it also impairs the organism's decision-making, imagination, and quality of life. This is perhaps especially true of the vmPFC and its role in the dopamine circuit.

Before we outline the precise function of the vmPFC, we shall outline a modern perspective on Freudian dream theory in order to contrast it with more contemporary data on the actual function of the vmPFC.

Boag (2006) attempts to legitimate Freudian dream theory by defining repression as inhibition and arguing that the function of the vmPFC is behavioral inhibition, and that during sleep the vmPFC acts as Freud's "dream-censor", constructing the bizarreness of the dream-world by way of dream-censorship:

"Solms equates the ventromedial frontal cortex with "executive inhibition . . . of which censorship is a special variety" (Solms, 1999, p. 192; cf. Kaplan-Solms & Solms, 2000, pp. 230–231). The problem here, according to Braun (1999), is that the ventromedial frontal cortex is said to be both the "censoring" part of the brain while also constituting the area of the brain involved with "wishes": "It seems odd that he [Solms] places the seat of the appetitive drives and craving in the same tissue as the behavioural censor" (Braun, 1999, p. 200). Thus, Braun believes that there is a contradiction here, since "censoring" and "motivation" should be physiologically distinct. However, as the account of repression presented here demonstrates, a relationship between motivation and "censoring" (inhibiting) would, in fact, be predicted. Repression involves motivational conflict, not a distinct "censor", and "censoring" is just as motivationally driven as the "forbidden wish" (i.e., there is no difference in kind between a wish that p occur and a wish that p not occur). In fact, since inhibition occurs in relation to motivational conflict, it would be expected that the areas of the brain associated with inhibition would also be areas associated with motivation. Solms is accordingly justified in making such a connection." (Boag, 2006, p. 12)

We believe that Braun (1999) is correct in identifying an inconsistency in Solms's thought in this regard, that "censoring" and "motivation" should be physiologically distinct.

Even if we take a more equivocal stance and locate censoring and motivation in the same structure, there remains a qualitative difference between "censoring", or fear response, and motivation, such that the two, even when provoked by the same object, are differentiated in subjective experience, and do not take the form of an undifferentiated "forbidden wish". We shall return to this latter point in our discussions of the amygdala and the dopamine circuit.

Moreover, although it is true that "inhibition occurs in relation to motivational conflict", the vmPFC is neither the site of inhibition nor motivational conflict.

According to a study by Winecoff et al. (2013), the function of the vmPFC is to encode emotional value. Studies which claim that the role of the vmPFC is inhibition (behavioral inhibition, cognitive control, emotion regulation, reappraisal, etc.) examine activity in the vmPFC only during the regulation of *negative* affects, leaving open the possibility that "the increased signal in the vmPFC reflects the change in emotional value after emotion regulation" (Winecoff et al., 2013, p.11032). To resolve the role of the vmPFC, Winecoff et al. (2013) examined brain activity with fMRI during subjects' regulation of either positive or negative affects. The results indicated that there is "a clear reduction in vmPFC activation during the *regulation* of positive emotion compared with the *experience* of positive emotion" (Winecoff et al., 2013, 11037; emphasis my own). There is less activity in the vmPFC during the *regulation* of positive emotion, suggesting that the vmPFC is not responsible for "executive inhibition" or for "censoring".

Winecoff et al. (2013), summarizing their own and others' research, write that:

"Studies of reward processing have implicated the vmPFC in the valuation of rewards from various modalities…These studies support the idea that vmPFC computes a domain-general appetitive value signal (Roy et al., 2012) manifest in our own data as emotional reward value. In other words, our results indicate that two sorts of value, responses to rewards and to the emotional content of images, are tracked similarly in vmPFC along continuous scales." (p. 11037)

The regulation of emotion, on the other hand, is caused by the dorsolateral prefrontal cortex (dlPFC): "Subjects who successfully implemented self-control evinced increased activation in the dlPFC…and decreased activation in the vmPFC" (Winecoff et al., 2013, p. 11038). So it is the dlPFC, not the vmPFC, which is responsible for "executive inhibition":

"The dlPFC signal in the regulation condition might reflect computations that are ultimately integrated into the final encoding of value (e.g., context). Participants in our regulation condition attempted to emotionally detach themselves from the images (i.e., to neutralize emotional responses). Therefore, achieving the goal of regulation might contribute to an integrated neural signal for value." (Winecoff et al., 2013, p. 11038).

Braun (1999) is entirely justified in concluding that there is a contradiction to Solms's justification of Freudian dream theory. Boag's (2006) claim that Freudian dream theory is corroborated by neuroscience is a bogus claim. The re-discovery of the importance of the vmPFC to dreaming, which can be attributed to Solms (2000), itself refutes Freudian dream theory, given that the function of the vmPFC is encoding emotional value and that "executive inhibition" is controlled by a different component of the brain, the dlPFC. It must also be recalled, as we have written above, that there is *less* activity in the dlPFC during REM (in which the majority of dreams occur) (Stickgold et al., 2001, p. 1056). Stickgold et al. (2001) write that this "inhibits the ability of DLPFC to allocate attentional resources" (p. 1056), but as we have seen, it also inhibits the ability of the dlPFC to perform "executive inhibition". Solms (2000) himself writes that lesions to the dlPFC have no effect on dreaming, and that therefore activity in the dlPFC, which he acknowledges is responsible for executive control, is inessential to dreaming (p. 848). A double negative, meaning that there is more executive freedom (or *freedom of expression*, if you will) in dreams than in waking life due to decreased activity in the dlPFC during REM sleep. Dream-bizarreness in part arises due to *freedom of expression*, or more precisely, *dream-freedom-of-expression*:

"What is certain is that this enfolding, through the medium of which eternity becomes liveable to us, is not produced in dreams in the same way as in life. Something of this fold unfolds. Thanks to this our limits change, widen. The past, the future no longer exist; the dead rise again; places construct themselves without architect, without journeys, without that tedious oppression that compels us to live minute by minute that which the half-opened fold shows us at a glance. Moreover the atmospheric and profound triviality of the dream favours encounters, surprises, acquaintanceships, a naturalness which our enfolded world (I mean projected onto the surface of a fold) can only ascribe to the supernatural." (Cocteau, 1946/1966)

While we dream, the reality of the dream world appears natural to us. On waking, it is bizarre, "supernatural". The "supernatural" quality of dreams arises from the ease with which there is an *apparent* freedom of movement, an *apparent* freedom from the laws of physics, an *apparent* freedom from history and death, in dreams. In dreams, any place or any being may be involuntarily conjured by the unconscious. This is only an apparent freedom, however, since the brain remains encultured and made of matter, and thus subject to the laws of physics and biology, as well as confined to the symbolic universe of its socio-cultural milieu. The "profound triviality" of dreams is their socially constructed nature (the dream-images as involuntary social constructions, or social productions, of our unconscious; the social production of (virtual) reality). These apparent freedoms arise from the dreaming brain's freedom of expression. Indeed, the freedom of expression of the unconscious during dreams is often a terrifying freedom. Consciousness finds itself involuntarily trapped in a world produced unconsciously by the mind, without knowing that the world in which it is trapped is illusory.

One wonders if by using the image of folds, of enfoldings and unfoldings, whether Cocteau is alluding to and metaphorizing the folds of the cortex. Cocteau notices that the "tedious oppression that compels us to live minute by minute" are absent in dreams, all the minute details and boredom which are the natural part of the "slow" passage of time during waking life are absent in dreams, and that dreams favour "encounters, surprises, acquaintanceships", i.e., emotionally salient stimuli; this may be because of the prominent role of the vmPFC in dreaming, which, since its function is to encode emotional stimuli, would produce a dream-world in which emotionally salient stimuli are favoured. However, we note that boring dreams may occur in cases where boredom itself serves as a salient emotion.

Solms is more accurate in his later view that there is "no need to introduce the additional function of censorship", and that dream-bizarreness is due to "the mere fact that the system is forced to function in the way that it does, where the executive systems of the frontal lobes cannot program, regulate, and verify the output of the posterior forebrain"; in short, that Freud's hypothesis of dream-censorship "may have been wrong" (Solms and Turnbull, 2002, p. 215). Solms and Turnbull (2002), however, maintain that there is a distinction between "latent" (unconscious) and "manifest" (conscious) content of dreams (pp. 214-215). However, with evidence against dream-censorship there is no basis for arguing that such a distinction may be made, just as, as we have discussed earlier, one cannot make a distinction between what is conscious and unconscious on the basis of repression because repression does not exist.

The function of the vmPFC is clearly defined:

"In summary, our results indicate that the vmPFC does not act as a control region during emotion regulation, but rather encodes the affective value of emotional stimuli along a continuous scale. Our results point to an adaptive, flexible computation of value: conditional factors such as emotion regulation affect how emotional value signals are encoded in the vmPFC." (Winecoff et al., 2013, 11038).

The findings of Winecoff et al. (2013) offer a fresh perspective with which to examine the relation of the vmPFC to adynamia and to emotional learning. As we wrote in an earlier section, decision-making depends upon emotions, and emotional impairments also impair decision-making. In the Iowa Gambling Task experiment, subjects with lesions to certain areas are distinguished from healthy subjects by their capacity for emotional learning, the prerequisite of rational decision-making in real-time; one of the brain areas necessary for emotional learning and rational decision-making is the vmPFC, damage to which impairs the capacity to feel emotions and the capacity to reason (Damasio, 1994; Bechara, Damasio, Damasio, and Lee, 1999).

Emotional learning is a form of associative learning. Associations are formed through emotional learning, through the encoding of emotional stimuli. The major role of a structure responsible for a form of associative learning (the vmPFC) in dreams explains why an area responsible for mental imagery, quasi-spatial symbolic operations, and symbol processing (the PTO junction) would also play a major role in dreaming. The PTO junction provides the stimuli which the vmPFC encodes emotionally. When the vmPFC is intact, lesions to the PTO junction result in the cessation of dreaming because then the vmPFC has no stimuli to encode. The encoding of emotional stimuli is so essential to the function of dreams that in the case of extensive damage to the vmPFC dreams cease altogether, even though the source of dream-images (the PTO junction) remains intact.

Emotional learning is the function of dreams and dreaming.
Emotional learning is synonymous to the encoding of emotional stimuli; thus, it is consistent that with vmPFC damage, emotional learning becomes impossible. Damasio (1994) does not indicate whether the patients with vmPFC damage whom he investigates dream or not, but other evidence he presents suggests that they probably do not.

Damasio's (1994) patient Elliot, whose vmPFC is lesioned, is described as having reduced interest, reduced initiative, and reduced ability to plan ahead, which are characteristics of an impaired dopamine circuit. Although Elliot's lack of initiative is not specifically called adynamia, it sufficiently resembles adynamia to be described by that epithet:

"Consider the beginning of his [Elliot's] day: He needed prompting to get started in the morning and prepare to go to work. Once at work he was unable to manage his time properly; he could not be trusted with a schedule. When the job called for interrupting an activity and turning to another, he might persist nonetheless, seemingly losing sight of his main goal." (Damasio, 1994, p. 36)

Although Elliot is described by Damasio (1994) as highly intelligent, he nonetheless suffers from adynamia. His will is weakened, such that he is taken advantage of by others who realize his condition: "In one enterprise, he teamed up with a disreputable character. Several warnings from friends were of no avail, and the scheme ended in bankruptcy. All of his savings had been invested in the ill-fated enterprise and all were lost" (p. 37). This is the same helpless state that leukotomy patients, or rather victims, were reduced to, and that antipsychotics eventually reduce people to. As it relates to dreaming, "adynamia (a common side effect of the surgical transection of this circuit) is a typical correlate of loss of dreaming following deep bifrontal lesions, and it statistically discriminates between dreaming and nondreaming patients with such lesions" (Solms, 2000, p. 847). When the damage to the vmPFC is extensive enough to cause adynamia, it also causes loss of dreaming.

What Elliot and other subjects with lesions to the vmPFC cannot do while awake, they also cannot do while asleep: emotional learning.

Furthermore, there is no "latent", content of dreams. Dreams, more so than waking consciousness, are pure surface: appearances have an immediate and direct effect on dream-consciousness, unclouded by latent meanings which executive control might insert into them. Of course, the source of the images which constitute dreams is our own memories, which, due to their not being immediately accessible to consciousness, may be described as unconscious, but they are in no way unconscious in the Freudian sense. There is no unconscious hidden theater in which memories are re-enacted beneath the surface of the dream-world. Memories in dreams, far from remaining unconscious as the "latent" content of dreams, directly constitute the appearances of the dream-world. The unconscious *produces* the dream-world, like a factory, projecting dream-images upon our dreaming consciousness, a pure surface, using memories and associations stored in the cortex; the dream is a film in which consciousness is both actor and spectator. The unconscious harbors the *pre-conditions* of dream-images and its *operations* directly produce the dream-world. But there is no "latent dream" occurring behind or beneath the dream which appears to consciousness. In other words, in dreams the "meanings" of memories—*affective meanings*—are *made conscious*, since their affective meanings, their emotional significance, is rendered directly accessible to consciousness.

We may glean a clearer insight into the nature of the dream-images as they relate to affective meanings if we consider the following passage by Sartre (1943/1956), which, taken out of its original context, can be read as descriptive of the dream-world:

"In the first place we certainly thus get rid of that dualism which in the existent opposes interior to exterior. There is no longer an exterior for the existent if one means by that a superficial covering which hides from sight the true nature of the object. And this true nature in turn, if it is to be the secret reality of the thing, which one can have a presentiment of or which one can suppose but can never reach because it is the "interior" of the object under consideration— this nature no longer exists...The obvious conclusion is that the dualism of being and appearance is no longer entitled to any legal status within philosophy. The appearance refers to the total series of appearances and not to a hidden reality which would drain to itself all the *being* of the existent...For the being of an existent is exactly what it *appears*...What it is, it is absolutely, for it reveals itself as it is. The phenomenon can be studied and described as such, for it is *absolutely indicative of itself."* (pp. 3-4)

The equivalence of being and appearance described by Sartre (1943/1956) in the above passage holds true, in an exact corresponding way, to dream-images and their affective meanings. There is no "secret reality" of the dream which has a transcendent, paramount status as reality and which determines the "manifest" content of dreams. There is neither a "latent" nor a "manifest" content of dreams. In dreams, the only content is the content which appears: the dream-images and their corresponding affects in the subject. Through emotional learning, the dreaming subject, who is conscious throughout the dream, is being taught approach-avoidance behaviors by the sleeping brain.

The "meaning" of dreams are neither divine nor Oedipal. The meanings of dreams are *affective meanings. Affective meaning* is how Roy, Shohamy, and Wager (2012) describe the function of the vmPFC:

"The vmPFC thus functions as a hub that links concepts with brainstem systems capable of coordinating organism-wide emotional behavior, a process we describe in terms of the generation of *affective meaning,* and which could explain the common role played by the vmPFC in a range of experimental paradigms." (p. 147; emphasis my own)

The vmPFC directly mediates stimuli, "representations" or "signs", to consciousness (the PAG), assigning affects to signs so that consciousness experiences the aggregate as an association (of affect with stimuli). It must be remembered that affects themselves consist of signs (interoceptive representations). Therefore, the dream-images which present themselves to consciousness signify affects (the aggregate of signs which *are* affects), and these affects in conjunction with the dream-images constitute dream-consciousness; thus, the signs which constitute dream-consciousness (the affects and their corresponding stimuli) form both the surface and the "meaning" of dreams.

Emotional learning, the processing of affective meanings, is a complex form of associative learning which has evolutionary advantages because it allows the organism to adapt to novel or rapidly changing events based upon the "precise configuration" of salient stimuli:

"To summarize, building on extensive data regarding the role of vmPFC in subjective value, affect, memory and visceromotor control, we propose that meaning-guided affect as represented in vmPFC is a) *generative* and can be easily transferred to new situations or configurations of informational elements; b) shows *sensitive* dependence to the precise configuration of elements, but not to incidental variations in sensory appearance; and c) can *change rapidly* during learning. This view of affective meaning is closely aligned with the idea that 'affective appraisal' and 'situated conceptualization' are critical emotion-generating processes, and with other dual-process views that suggest that 'model-based' or 'goal-directed' systems operate alongside simpler habit learning systems to guide reward-driven learning in animals. Unlike simpler forms of learning and valuation, affective meaning arises from the fast recombination of conceptual information extracted from long-term memory into predictive models of the self in context, which drive both decision-making and physiological affective responses. This highly integrative process appears to rely on the vmPFC, which binds together large-scale networks involved in several functions that are necessary to construct affective meaning: memory and future projection, self-perception, social cognition, emotion, reward, and autonomic and endocrine function." (Roy, Shohamy, and Wager, 2012, p. 154)

The three attributes of emotional learning which Roy, Shohamy, and Wager (2012) sketch have obvious connections to the dream-world. Dreams are a) generative, since the brain generates novel situations and configurations of signs, b) sensitive and dependent "to the precise configuration" of signs, since a novel event (a novel configuration of signs) alters the dream unpredictably, and c) change rapidly, so much so that one may simply turn in a circle in a dream and find one's self on a new planet. It is the three attributes of emotional learning, which is the function of the vmPFC, which are embodied in the dream-world because of the vmPFC's prominent role in dreaming. Dreams are produced by the "fast recombination of conceptual information [signs] extracted from long-term memory", and the dream-world is a predictive model "of the self in context", in which the subject experiences scenarios of decision-making driven by "physiological affective responses". The "highly integrative process" of dreaming is due not only to the symbol-processing PTO junction, but also due to the vmPFC, which is "necessary to construct affective meaning" because it "binds together large-scale networks involved in several functions" such as "memory and future projection, self-perception, social cognition, emotion, reward, and autonomic and endocrine function".

In conclusion, dreams are a biological phenomenon which are organically produced by biological structures of the brain, and therefore dreaming arose by natural selection because dreamers have an evolutionary advantage over non-dreamers. The evolutionary advantage and function of dreams, which, using the clinico-anatomical correlation method, can be inferred by the prominent role of the vmPFC during dreams (even independent of REM sleep), is that while asleep, a process of associative learning, more specifically the form of associative learning known as emotional learning, can occur in the relative absence of exteroceptive sensory stimuli and the absence of motile activity of the body.

A Dream Within A Dream, Part II: The Dopaminergic Basis of Dreaming

Our theory of dreams as emotional learning is complete: it accounts for both positive dreams and nightmares, and it accounts for the recurring nightmares often experienced during PTSD. It is also further corroborated by the role of certain other structures in REM sleep and by the dopaminergic basis of dreaming. The dopaminergic basis of dreaming explains the entire emotional spectrum of dreams, including nightmares, and it disproves Freud's claim that dreams are essentially wish-fulfillment. The vmPFC, which is part of the brain's dopamine (DA) circuit, is able to encode both negative and positive affectual stimuli because dopamine is responsible for both desire and dread.

Although Panksepp characterizes the DA system as the "seeking system", desire is only one function of the DA system; the other is dread. The results of Faure et al. (2008) indicate that "dopamine participates in *parallel channels* of mesocorticolimbic signals that are oppositely valenced to generate desire versus dread" (p.7190; emphasis my own). (A side note: Faure et al. (2008) furnish their results by modulating dopamine in the nucleus accumbens, long considered to be the brain's "pleasure center" or "reward center"; just as with the amygdala, often mistakenly described as the brain's "fear center", this is an oversimplification and misrepresentation of the actual functions of the nucleus accumbens). In addition, Fadok, Dickerson, and Palmiter (2009) found that "dopamine is necessary for cue-dependent fear conditioning".

Fear and desire have intimately parallel existences; the same neurotransmitter can trigger affective states (involving either pleasure or pain) and corresponding behaviours (approach or avoidance) which are distinct and qualitatively opposed to each other. Even when there is a little fear in desire or a little desire in fear, fear and desire are not experienced as a non-differentiated unity, but they retain their qualitative differences in subjective experience, leading to a play of affective states and approach and avoidance behaviors. The DA system *does* serve the function of a "seeking system", but it *also* serves the function of a "fear system", and though these two systems are parallel to each other, they are two distinct systems.

Although Panksepp does outline a "FEAR system", he identifies its key neurotransmitters as Neuropeptide Y and corticotropin releasing factor (CRF, also called corticotropin releasing hormone, CRH) (Panksepp, 2010). Panksepp also describes his "FEAR system" as the "anxiety system", since GABAergic drugs are used to treat anxiety disorders (Panksepp, 2010). What Panksepp describes as the "FEAR system" (at least when it comes to neurotransmitters involved), we would describe, perhaps more accurately, as the "stress system", due to the fact that CRF and adrenocorticotropic hormone (ACTH) are released in response to stress (Kalat, 2016, pp. 383-384). On the other hand, dopamine can activate instinctive fear responses (Faure et al., 2008), therefore the "fear system" is more accurately characterized as a function of the DA system.

Although dopamine is potentially reinforcing, as evinced by the addictive potential of dopaminergic drugs such as cocaine and methamphetamine, the role of dopamine is not limited to that of a reinforcer. Dopamine also has major roles in desire (the active, "seeking" or wanting of desire, not its consummation) and in dread. This is reflected in dreams, in which one may experience shades of a range of feelings, including nightmares, and in which one may or may not obtain the object of desire (in dreams which are driven by desire). Freud's hypothesis that dreams are essentially wish-fulfillment is far too simplistic a model, as it does not account for the richness and variety of our subjective experience of dreams.

Furthermore, the dopaminergic basis of dreaming also explains the "mystical" or "supernatural" quality of dreams, which, though not frequently discussed in scientific literature, is often discussed in art and religion. Religiosity, religious practice in healthy individuals, and religious experiences all involve the DA circuit and the mesocorticolimbic system, including the amygdala and the prefrontal cortex (McNamara, 2009, pp. 108-129). Overactivity in these same structures and neurotransmitter system is a correlate or cause of many of the positive symptoms of "schizophrenia"; chemically activating the DA circuit "stimulates not only positive psychotic symptoms but also excessive, unusually vivid dreaming and nightmares" (Solms, 2000, p. 847). Religious experience, and even religiosity, involve positive symptoms of schizophrenia; the former is indistinguishable from a psychotic episode and the latter is indistinguishable from delusional disorder.

Religious experiences are characterized by hallucinations and delusions. Religiosity, often correlated with religious practices, consists of delusions. Delusions, parsimoniously defined, are "false beliefs about the world that persist tenaciously despite repeated encounters with contradicting evidence" (Wang and Krystal, 2014, p.644). Gods, goddesses, immortal souls, angels, demons, and other metaphysical substances cannot be empirically proven to exist, and many commonly known facts as well as more obscure paradoxes observed by philosophers contradict the existence of these metaphysical entities. For example, anyone willing to experiment, using the scientific method, can discover for themselves that prayers do not by themselves put any actions into motion external to the self (as predicted by the hypothesis that a deity "answers" prayers), and in philosophy the Omnipotence Paradox, among many other arguments, disproves the existence of an omnipotent being. Whenever God is assumed to exist, contradictions are generated, such as the Omnipotence Paradox: "Can God create an object so heavy that even he cannot lift it? If he can create it, and cannot lift the object, then he is not all-powerful. If he cannot create it, then he is not all-powerful. Therefore, God is impotent." This contradiction means that there is an inconsistency with the hypothesis that an omnipotent being exists; since contradictions are generated when an omnipotent being is assumed to exist, it is safe to infer that omnipotent beings do not exist.

Furthermore, these metaphysical entities have no more objective existence than the metaphysical entities experienced by or posited to exist by someone who is hallucinating; this point is satirized quite aptly by Bobby Henderson's "Flying Spaghetti Monster". If a deity called, due to its purported appearance, the "Flying Spaghetti Monster", is posited to exist, and a mass of people decide to worship it, there is no objective basis for proving its existence, just like any other deity, and therefore it is just as legitimate, that is to say, illegitimate. To posit its existence is just as absurd as positing the existence of any other metaphysical entity, and the burden of proof does not lie with those who disbelieve such astonishing claims.

Faith proves nothing. Nietzsche (1881/1920) eloquently rendered this thought by writing: "the fact that faith actually moves no mountains, but instead raises them up where there were none before: all this is made sufficiently clear by a walk through a lunatic asylum" (p. 143). His words have been distilled by time and they are often quoted as "A casual stroll through a lunatic asylum shows that faith proves nothing." Subjective feelings or "intuitions" are not the same as the reality external to the self, and they may not correspond to the reality which exists independent of the self. Feelings are interoceptive, not exteroceptive.

Just as with schizophrenia and psychosis, religiosity may or may not be of a paranoid nature (God is punishing me, the Devil causing harm to me and others, etc.). Furthermore, statistically, people motivated by religious beliefs cause more harm to themselves and others than schizophrenics and psychotics (for example, Christian fundamentalists who bomb abortion centers and kill medical professionals, people who kill themselves because they believe they have "sinned", etc.), and this has historically always been the case (for example, holy wars and witch burnings). For a history of atrocities committed against the "insane" in the name of Christianity or Christian morals, we refer the reader to Michel Foucault's *History of Madness* (1961/2006).

It is a great and incredible hypocrisy of Western culture that schizophrenics and psychotics are treated with such stigma and are demonized and misrepresented by pop-culture and the media while the Christian religion, which like all religions consists of delusions, is so ardently praised, promoted, and enforced even by governments. For example, because of laws inspired by Christian fundamentalism, it is increasingly difficult for a woman to have an abortion, a medical procedure, in the United States. Who is it that is in actuality insane? The schizo, or the Christian?

And, of course, our belief in the dream-world as reality (while we dream) is also a matter of faith. Most often, a matter of blind faith, an unquestioning and uncritical belief. Every time we wake, we realize anew that the object of our faith, the dream-world, is illusory and ephemeral. It is precisely this perfect faith and its perfect dissolution upon waking that have provoked countless philosophers, including Chuang Chou, in questioning the reality of waking life, in which, for the most part, we also have perfect faith:

"Once Chuang Chou dreamt he was a butterfly, a butterfly flitting and fluttering around, happy with himself and doing as he pleased. He didn't know he was Chuang Chou. Suddenly he woke up and there he was, solid and unmistakable Chuang Chou. But he didn't know if he was Chuang Chou who had dreamt he was a butterfly, or a butterfly dreaming he was Chuang Chou. Between Chuang Chou and a butterfly there must be some distinction! This is called the Transformation of Things." (translated by Burton Watson, 1968)

We do not pretend to have exhausted the possible meanings of Chuang Chou's parable. We merely note that as a butterfly, Chuang Chou had perfect faith that he was a butterfly, a faith which was shattered when he woke up and found that he was Chuang Chou; but, as the reverse side of this movement, Chuang Chou lost his perfect faith that he was Chuang Chou, and he came to recognize "The Transformation of Things", and thus to embrace the uncertainty of being.

In the face of the daily destruction of a perfect faith which dreams bring, it is a miracle that people have faith in anything at all. In a way of speaking, reality *is* an illusion; following Berger and Luckmann (1967), we recognize that reality is socially constructed, and that socially constructed reality consists of the *symbolic universe* of a culture (an aggregate of signs).

People conceive of and experience as reality a mental model (or virtual reality) which is built with and upon culturally relative, socially acquired concepts; these concepts (or social constructs) and this model are unempirical and often do not correspond to empirical reality. A social construction, or a social construct, is a delusion. For example, all concepts of gods and goddesses are social constructs which, even though they have no objective existence, religious people may claim to feel inside of them or to perceive external to their self.

Richard Dawkins (2006), in his book *The God Delusion*, also argues that religious belief is delusional, but the view has older origins. Pirsig (1991) wrote: "When one person suffers from a delusion it is called insanity. When many people suffer from a delusion it is called religion" (as quoted in Dawkins, 2006, p. 406). And about a hundred years earlier, Karl Marx famously wrote that

"Religion is the opiate of the masses." Considering the dopaminergic basis of religious belief, perhaps it would be better to update Marx and say "Religion is the amphetamine of the masses."

The role of dopamine in religious belief and schizophrenia helps us to understand the dreamer, who also dreams in delusion, for the dreamer believes that they are awake, and that the world they are encountering in their dreams is reality. It is due to the illusory nature of the dream-world that we describe the dream-world as a "virtual reality"; activity in the DA circuit produces both the virtual reality and the belief that this virtual reality is the real one. Both the religious and the schizophrenic also have brains which produce virtual realities, or more precisely, their brains produce models of the world, the self, and others which, although they do not correspond to objective reality, they believe *to be* objective reality; just as with dreams, the DA circuit plays a crucial role in this production process.

However, our discussion, insofar as we have utilized the concept of schizophrenia/psychosis, is inadequate; schizophrenia is not a uniform or singular entity such that one can say definitively what a schizophrenic is. Furthermore, it has not been established whether a given individual who has been diagnosed as schizophrenic has a better or worse sense of empirical reality than a "normal" and "healthy" individual; considering the prevalence of religion, the "healthy" individual does not necessarily have an accurate sense of reality. We also argue that the psychiatrist, insofar as he believes that the categories of mental illness which have been taught to him are real, is also delusional, for he believes in delusions, and hence he is similar to those with religious faith and to the "schizophrenic". The pious psychiatrist lives just as much in an illusory world of his own construction as the "psychotic", and insofar as the psychiatrist believes in the socially constructed categories of mental illness which have been taught to him, he suffers from delusional disorder; insofar as the pious psychiatrist *perceives* these "mental illnesses", he is hallucinating, for these "mental illnesses" do not have any empirical, biological basis (we point to poor inter-rater reliability for diagnosing "mental illness" and the lack of biopathology), therefore the psychiatrist, too, suffers from "schizophrenia". Where is the *coherence* in the discourse of psychiatry? And is not its treatment of patients *aggressive?*, either passive-aggressive or an outright abusive destruction of brain systems?

A Dream Within A Dream, Part III: Auxiliary Brain Structures Which Are Likely Involved In Dreaming

Although REM and dreaming are dissociable states, they are intimately related, and given that most dreams occur during REM, it is likely that the mechanisms of REM facilitate the mechanisms of dreaming (Solms, 2000, p. 849). During REM sleep, the anterior cingulate cortex (ACC) and the amygdala become active at levels equal to or above waking levels (Stickgold et al., 2001, p. 1054). The ACC and the amygdala, like the vmPFC, are both part of the brain's dopamine circuit. In addition, they are both part of the mesocortico-mesolimbic system, which is known to be responsible for emotions.

The ACC is highly interconnected with the PFC, including both the vmPFC and the dlPFC (Paus, 2001). For some time, the ACC was thought to be responsible for cognitive control (the two theories which support the cognitive control hypothesis are the error-detection theory and the conflict-monitoring theory), but these two theories do not account for all observed instances of ACC activity and it also fails to distinguish between ACC and dlPFC activity (Paus, 2001, pp. 420-421). Rushworth et al. (2007) conclude that the ACC "mediates the relationship between the previous action-reinforcement history and the next action choice...At the same time, the ACC has a complementary role in the exploratory generation of actions to ascertain the reinforcement potential of a new situation" (p. 175). However, Paus (2001) ascribes a more prominent role of the ACC as responsible for the exploratory generation of actions:

"...the ACC seems to come into play when rehearsed actions are not sufficient to guide behaviour. The results of lesion and imaging studies support this idea: the lesion is more likely to interfere with the acquisition of a novel behaviour, and activation of the ACC is most frequently observed during the performance of unrehearsed actions." (p. 423)

Furthermore, the ACC encodes action-reinforcement representations, action values, and the probability of rewards (Rushworth et al., 2007, p. 169). Since during REM sleep, the dlPFC is inactive and the ACC is active, the role of the ACC during dreams cannot be executive control. Rather, the ACC is active in connection with the vmPFC, meaning that the ACC's function during dreams tends more towards emotional learning. The activation of the ACC during REM sleep suggests that dreams are not merely the repetition of memories, but also, in part, consist of novel experiences (based upon the recombination of episodic memories), in which novel behaviours are experienced (based upon the recombination of memories of past behaviours), since the ACC mediates past actions and future actions. During dreams, the vmPFC not only stimulates the recall of previously encoded stimuli, but also encodes new stimuli which the brain produces through syntheses of memory traces.

To be clear, episodic memories are indeed sometimes relived in dreams, but it is also the case that many of our dreams are new, "unrehearsed" experiences. The novelty of dreams accounts in part for dream-bizarreness. The other phenomenon which accounts for dream-bizarreness is freedom of expression, which in turn partially accounts for novelty. "Bizarreness", after all, is another way of saying "strangeness"; the dream world is one which, upon waking, appears altogether unfamiliar, that is to say, novel. Dream-bizarreness is accounted for by the dreaming brain's freedom of expression (executive freedom or lack of inhibitions) and its production of novel stimuli.

The ACC and the vmPFC are both highly interconnected with the amygdala (Rushworth et al., 2007, p. 169). As we have written in a previous section, damage to the amygdala impairs emotional processing and rational decision-making, which is in some ways comparable to damage to the vmPFC, especially if the impairment is measured via the Iowa Gambling Task (Damasio, 1994; Bechara, Damasio, Damasio, and Lee, 1999). Although the amygdala is often mentioned in connection to processing fear stimuli, this is only because that is the phenomenon which is the most well-studied in this brain structure; in reality, the amygdala processes a spectrum of emotions, from positive to negative (Phelps and Ledoux, 2005; Baird et al., 2003). In a different yet comparable way to the vmPFC, the amygdala is also responsible for emotional learning.

Amygdala size is positively correlated with sex drive (Baird et al., 2003). This finding is at first glance at odds with the studies of amygdala lesions, which results in the condition called Klüver-Bucy syndrome, which includes among its symptoms indiscriminate sexual behavior towards "inappropriate" objects. Baird et al. (2003) support the *distinction* between *increased* sexual behavior and *indiscriminate* sexual behavior:

"These behaviors [of Klüver-Bucy syndrome] are best interpreted as a "decrease in selectivity" of the target of sexual advances and the time and place of sexual expression. In contrast, the postoperative sexual increase described by our patients primarily consists of an increase in sex drive without indiscriminate sexual behavior." (p. 94)

It is important to remember that the amygdala is not the site of the sex drive as such, but serves the processing of emotional stimuli:

"One possibility is that a larger amygdala functions better in its role as a processor of emotional stimuli, specifically social/sexual cues, and in the attachment of significance to such stimuli. This would increase the likelihood of sexual response, resulting in a sexual increase." (Baird et al., 2003, p. 94)

And conversely, the lack of an amygdala would mean the inability to process social/sexual cues and the inability to assign valence to objects (and thus to form preferences), thus leading to indiscriminate sexual behavior. The position of Baird et al. (2003) is supported by the research of Damasio (1994) and Bechara, Damasio, Damasio, and Lee (1999) regarding the role of the amygdala in emotional learning.

Although the amygdala plays an important role in fear, sexual desire, and decision making, it is not the structure which is responsible for these things as such. The amygdala cannot even be said to be the brain's "fear center", as it is often characterized. Even subjects with lesions to the amygdala feel fear and have panic attacks when they inhale carbon dioxide (which signals to the brain that it is suffocating), including SM, the archetypal human case study of amygdala lesion (Feinstein et al., 2013). The amygdala is responsible for processing emotional stimuli—although the exact model of how it does so is unclear, it may function similarly to the vmPFC, encoding emotional value, or affective meaning—and this capability of the amygdala is what makes it crucial to fear-processing, sexual desire, and decision-making, as well as dreaming.

A Dream Within A Dream, Part IV: Conceptualizing the Neurobiology of Dreams

We may conceptualize the neurobiology of dreams by recalling the following passage from Cocteau's novel *Les Enfants Terribles* (1929/1957): "Dreams resound sometimes with footsteps, mindless, purposeful, like hers; dreams lend us a gait lighter than winged flight, a step able to combine the statue's weight of inorganic marble with the sub-aqueous freedom of a deep sea diver" (pp. 134-135). "Mindless" because the dream-world is produced involuntarily, without the volition of the conscious mind; "purposeful" because dreams are dopaminergic, driven either by desire or by dread. Dreams possess both "the statue's weight of inorganic marble" and "the sub-aqueous freedom of a deep sea diver" because of the diminished activity in the dlPFC, which is responsible for executive inhibition; unable to fully control ourselves in our dreams, we move as if driven by fate, with the dead weight of inorganic marble, but this lack of inhibitions simultaneously gives our minds a freedom of expression which allows it to take us places inaccessible to us when, while waking, we are in more control of ourselves. Hence dreams' "gait lighter than winged flight", "lighter than winged flight" because the gait of dreams is the flight of unconscious, cosmic wings, perhaps such as those of the butterfly of the butterfly effect of chaos mathematics.

A Dream Within A Dream, Part V: A Deconstruction of Dream-Censorship

Because Freud's theory of dreams does not correlate with the facts, it too is a delusion, just like religious belief. But like religious belief, psychoanalysis is not recognized as delusion by its believers; it is a shared delusion, that is to say, it is ideology. Ideology is a shared delusion which legitimates and maintains socially constructed reality. Psychoanalysis, even when used by leftist theoreticians, maintains the status quo of bourgeois-dominated societies because it rests upon ideological foundations and not empirical facts.

Freudian dream theory rests upon two mutually dependent hypotheses: that dreams are all wish-fulfillment, and that these wishes are disguised by the process of "dream-censorship". In the preceding section, Freud's ideas have been briefly mentioned, and the relevant facts which refute Freud's ideas have been elaborated upon. The divergence from facts well-established, we are now free to examine Freudian dream-theory from a sociological perspective and thus to examine their ideological basis.

Freud argues that dreams are wish-fulfillment on the basis of what he calls "linguistic usage", that is to say, from expressions which were in common usage in his time. Immediately, the break with empirical science is apparent. Instead of arguing from facts, Freud takes as his starting point folk psychology, accepting the folk psychology of his culture as fact:

"What animals dream of I do not know. There is a proverb, mentioned to me by one of my students, which claims to know, for it asks the question: *What does a goose dream of?* and answers: *Corn.* The entire theory that the dream is a wish-fulfillment is contained in these two sentences. We observe now that we would have found the shortest route to our theory of the hidden meaning of dreams if we had only looked to linguistic usage...in linguistic usage the dream is nevertheless the sweet fulfiller of wishes. 'I wouldn't have imagined it in my wildest dreams,' we cry in delight when we find our expectations surpassed reality." (Freud, 1899/1999, p. 105)

The phrase "I wouldn't have imagined it in my wildest dreams" is, of course, a cliché. Like all clichés, it does not describe our actual experience of the world—it trivializes our experience by stuffing it into a facile category, thereby preventing us from reflecting on our actual experience (Proust often comments on this attribute of the cliché in his novel *Remembrance of Things Past*). Freud placidly accepts this cliché; instead of questioning it he legitimates it, giving it the weight of "science". For social theory, the 20th century has been the century of psychoanalysis, and philosophers such as Zizek drag this relic of the 19th century into the 21st; social theoreticians influenced by psychoanalysis have approached culture as wish-fulfillment, "fantasy" in the psychoanalytic sense. While wish-fulfillment may in part explain social phenomena, its role has been grossly over-exaggerated, resulting in the over-looking of other, perhaps more salient, precise, and predictive explanations. Critical analysis of culture, especially the analysis of ideology, is "sociology of knowledge"—if social constructs serve as the foundation for a sociology of knowledge, the problem is obvious: we are trapped in the confinements of the symbolic universe of a particular culture and we do not arrive at empirical knowledge. (For the same reason, Berger and Luckmann's (1967) reliance on phenomenology in *The Social Construction of Reality* is highly misleading).

Psychoanalytic interpretation is formulaic and facile; its ease of use has allowed its widespread diffusion in culture, such that Freudian ideas such as "oral fixation" or describing someone as "anal" are in everyday usage. Freud's ideas permeate the symbolic universe of Western society—they are experienced as knowledge and reality, even though they lack an empirical basis. Psychoanalysis is as easy as asking "What does a goose dream of?" and answering "Corn". After one asserts that there is a wish being fulfilled, one goes on to fit all subsequent facts into the model of wish-fulfillment, interpreting everything which does not fit with ease as "resistance" or "dream-distortion", thereby preserving the integrity of the model, which has replaced reality. Psychoanalysis is reification: the model it asserts takes the place of empirical reality, and facts are altered or "interpreted" in order to fit the model.

Freud's (1899/1999) theory of dreams is that all dreams are wish-fulfillment, but that the wishes are disguised by *dream-censorship*, also called *dream-distortion* (to refer to the distortion of dreams by a censor), and thus we arrive at the bizarre imagery of dreams, which only psychoanalysis can discover *the* truth of; the dream-imagery are disguised memories from early childhood, especially those of Oedipal infantile sexuality. Freud (1923/1960) writes that the ego "goes to sleep at night, though even then it exercises the censorship on dreams" (p. 7). As we have seen, empirical evidence invalidates the existence of an ego and the dream-censorship which purportedly follows from it.

In *The Interpretation of Dreams*, Freud (1899/1999) compares dream-censorship to political censorship:

"The correspondence, traceable down to the last detail, between the phenomena of censorship and dream-distortion justifies us in assuming similar preconditions for both. Accordingly we would assume two psychical forces (currents, systems) to be the originators of dream-formation in the individual; one of these forms the wish uttered by the dream, while the other imposes a censorship on the dream-wish and by this censorship distorts its expression." (p. 113)

In a letter to Fliess, Freud explicitly compares dream-censorship to the censorship by the Russian bourgeoisie and aristocracy, who blacked-out large sections of foreign newspapers so that foreign ideas threatening to their rule would not reach the populace:

"Have you ever seen a foreign newspaper which has passed Russian censorship at the frontier? Words, whole clauses and sentences are blacked out so that the rest becomes unintelligible. A *Russian censorship* of this kind comes about in psychoses and produces the apparently meaningless *deliria*." (Letter to Fliess dated 22 December 1897, in Masson, 1985, p. 289, emphasis in original; cf. Freud, 1900, p. 529; as quoted in Boag, 2006, p. 6)

Freud also refers to the censor as a "watchman" (Boag, 2006, p. 6).

It is important to note that political censorship and dream-censorship are not used by Freud as merely an analogy: their correspondence to each other are "traceable down to the last detail", and just as importantly, they are asserted to have similar preconditions. The preconditions of political censorship are the suppression of political freedoms, rigid and arbitrary morals, ethnocentrism, state-sanctioned or endogenously generated propaganda, and the systematic exploitation of the working class. The preconditions of dream-censorship—that is to say, the preconditions of psychoanalysis—are the same; it is towards these preconditions that Freud points to when he describes dream-censorship as the intra-psychological equivalent of political censorship. Although Freud was likely unaware of the ideological nature of psychoanalysis, the empirical socio-historical origins and uses of psychoanalysis also point towards these preconditions; we have already discussed briefly how the analyst crushes resistance.

In Freud's model of the mind, the ego is a bourgeois homunculus in our heads which makes sure that nothing will offend our conservative sensibilities, even in our dreams; even though dreams are the "sweet fulfiller of wishes", it appears that they never give us full satisfaction of our desires because the ego moderates the content of dreams, just like the MPAA perversely and obsessively moderates how many seconds of nudity may appear in a rated-R film. Freudian dream theory is just like a Hollywood film: your wishes are fulfilled but not really, some enjoyment is allowed as long as any excessive enjoyment is suppressed, and in the end it all leads back to maintaining existing power structures.

The ego, which is the agent which censors, is a "watchman", i.e., a policeman. The ego, in turn, is policed by the superego. In Freud's model, the superego consists of residues of a hypothetically infinite series of egos which can be traced backwards genealogically. The bourgeois homunculi multiply exponentially, and we are left with a brain full of policemen. Of course, empirically, the ego and the super-ego do not exist. But when the patient undergoes analysis, the analyst indoctrinates the patient into the religion of psychoanalysis and oedipalizes him or her, and through this process of oedipalization the patient internalizes or interiorizes the concepts of ego and super-ego, thereby setting up cognitive processes which fulfill the functions of ego and super-ego, namely self-censorship and self-policing. Eventually, as the interiorized ego and super-ego become automatized, they become activated unconsciously.

Frank Zappa and the Mothers of Invention ask, in a song, "Who Are the Brain Police?" We may answer that the ego and the superego, and more broadly, psychoanalysis and psychoanalysts, are the brain-police. The brain-police may already be at work in our minds without our being aware of it. The ideas of psychoanalysis (and their antecedent assumptions, which have older roots) permeate contemporary culture in the East and West.

There is, then, a two-fold sociopolitical repression or appropriation which occurs with psychoanalytic interpretation. First, the sociopolitical repression and appropriation of motivation, or "wishes". Our motives become no longer our own—they are dictated to us by the analyst, who follows directly, or through mediation by other theoreticians, the writings of Freud. Our wishes, whether ours or given to us by the analyst, are never fulfilled—they are forever inhibited to some degree by the brain-police, the ego and the superego. The wish becomes a pseudo-wish, diminished and impotent. Moreover, any given wish becomes combined with counter-wishes; counter-wishes are invoked to account for deficiencies in psychoanalytic explanations, there are counter-wishes motivating dream-censorship and repression (Boag, 2006, pp. 9-10). In this way, for example, Freud attempts to account for anxiety dreams: "The Freudian account of anxiety dreams is similarly explained in terms of "counter-wish dreams" (Freud, 1900, p. 157) where "the non-fulfilment of one wish meant the fulfilment of another" (Freud, 1900, p. 151; cf. Freud, 1916–17, p. 219)" (quotes and citations from Boag, 2006, p. 9). This makes Freudian dream theory similar to geocentrism: just as epicycles in geocentric models of the cosmos were posited to "correct" the inaccurate predictions of geocentric models, counter-wishes are posited in psychoanalysis to "correct" the inaccurate predictions of Freudian dream-theory. With the Freudian system of interpretation, all possibilities are accounted for, but there is no predictive value; any given phenomenon can be explained away by fitting it into the model by way of positing wishes and counter-wishes, but this same system makes it so that all possibilities and their counter-possibilities are equally valid hypotheses, which is an obviously impossible situation. Through psychoanalysis, especially through oedipalization, the mind becomes populated by the wishes and counter-wishes of brain-police. The second sociopolitical repression or appropriation, which we have already briefly discussed, is the transformation of the brain into a police state through the interiorization of the ego and superego which occurs during oedipalization.

Although Boag (2006) invokes the wish/counter-wish dichotomy as a "conflict of motivations" theory of repression which he envisions as separate from Freud's homuncular vision of the mind containing multiple ghost-like entities, it is much more consistent with Freud's theories if wishes and counter-wishes are attributed to homuncular agents (ego, id, superego). Thus, Boag's (2006) defense of Freud is neither supported by neuroscience nor is it an accurate account of Freud's theories; Boag (2006) himself cites many passages by Freud which describes dream-censorship as issuing from an agent-like censor, and as we have already mentioned, Freud hypothesized repression and dream-censorship as proceeding from the ego.

In summary, we agree with Hobson and Pace-Schott (1999) that:

"The hypothetical censor, which makes fine distinctions between acceptable and unacceptable wishes, is imbued by psychoanalysts with powers incompatible with its hypothesized weakened condition in sleep especially given the now replicated relative inactivity of executive frontal areas in both REM and NREM sleep." (Hobson and Pace-Schott, 1999, p. 208; as quoted in Boag, 2006, pp. 12-13)

Thus, it is apparent that there is a discrepancy between Freudian dream theory and the empirical facts of dreaming. This discrepancy suggests that Freudian dream theory is an example of socially constructed knowledge (or socially constructed reality), having as its basis the concepts and motives, both conscious and unconscious, of a socio-cultural milieu. Since socio-cultural milieus have more or less well-defined socio-political and socio-economic interests, the concepts and motives of a given socio-cultural milieu maintain those interests, therefore their concepts and motives can be accurately described by the label ideology. In short, psychoanalysis is a bourgeois ideology because it furthers the interests of the bourgeoisie and maintains their domination of the populace. Here we have presented a brief preliminary sketch of a sociology of psychoanalysis, by no means comprehensive nor complete. Psychoanalysis is already inherently political, since it assumes the existence of censors in the brain which Freud himself compares to political censors. As such, psychoanalysis is a tool of social control, not medical treatment. Furthermore, the use of psychoanalysis for the analysis of discourse, due to the foundations of psychoanalysis, cannot help but be ideological in nature; whether or not it is used by left-wing or right-wing thinkers, the psychoanalysis of discourse and the discourse of psychoanalysis are tantamount to the production of ideology which maintains the status quo, namely the exploitation of the working classes and the rule of the bourgeoisie.

A Dream Within A Dream, Part VI: Beware of the Dreams of Others

Although we have duly described the importance of emotional learning, we wish to make clear that we have not been singing its praises; there is a dark side to it. Also, the facts concerning the importance of emotional learning in psychic life have a potential to be exploited by an ideology of emotions which praises an anti-intellectual emotionality (the logical error here being that activities of the intellect are driven by emotions; thus anti-intellectualism also means opposition to a certain class of emotions), as has often ironically been the counterpoint of the ideology of reason, of cool reason holding the hot emotions in check like a dog on a leash—the two ideologies are not truly opposed to each other, for they both sustain the same society and ascribe to the same false dichotomy between reason and emotion. The dark side of emotional learning is that it allows us to learn *as if true* the ideas of our socio-cultural milieu, ideas which shape our thoughts, brains, and actions despite being false.

Since all experiences of emotions are conscious, there are no unconscious experiences of emotions; hence, no Freudian theater of the unconscious in which the eternal return of Oedipus is re-enacted. As Deleuze and Guattari (1972/1977) write, the unconscious is a factory which uses signs as its "raw materials" in the production process. To say that the unconscious uses signs to produce is the same as saying that it uses associations, because associations consist of signs.

Cognitive scientists make the distinction between explicit memories and implicit memories. Explicit memories are conscious, implicit memories unconscious. Our memories, our learned associations, are largely implicit, or unconscious. In this way, the cognitive load of our working memory, what we experience as the "present", is reduced. But the cost is that we are prone to prediction errors when our implicit associations do not correlate with objective reality. The occurrence of prediction errors in our daily lives is much more frequent than we typically assume. Indeed, social psychologists find that the average person considers themselves smarter than the average person, which cannot statistically be true, since the average person is, after all, by definition average, which is a polite way of saying mediocre (Kassin et al., 2014, p. 84).

Perhaps the most effective illustration of prediction errors caused by implicit associations is implicit prejudice. Kassin et al. (2014) makes a distinction between *prejudice* and *discrimination* (p. 155). Kassin et al. (2014) defines prejudice as "negative feelings about others because of their connection to a social group", and he defines discrimination as "negative behaviors directed against persons because of their membership in a particular group" (p. 155). For this section, we use the same distinction as Kassin et al. (2014). We are focusing our current discussion on prejudice, the negative feelings or attitudes which a given subject possesses against a particular social group. Some scholars recognize that there are two forms of prejudice, *explicit prejudice* and *implicit prejudice* (Kassin et al., 2014, pp. 157-159; Wilson and Scior, 2014; Greenwald et al., 1998). Explicit prejudice is prejudice that the subject is aware of possessing. By contrast, implicit prejudice is unconscious and the subject is unaware of it (Kassin et al., 2014, p. 157-159; Wilson and Scior, 2014; Greenwald et al., 1998). Greenwald and Banaji (1995) define "implicit attitudes", which we refer to in our study as "implicit prejudice", as "introspectively unidentified (or inaccurately identified) traces of past experience that mediate favorable or unfavorable feeling, thought, or action toward social objects" (p.8). In other words, implicit prejudice is an observable production of judgements or evaluations which are activated automatically, without the subject's awareness of the judgements and evaluations and their causes (Greenwald and Banaji, 1995, pp. 6-8). Implicit prejudices are automatically activated, without any effort or intention by the subject (Prestwich et al., 2008). Explicit prejudice is typically measured using self-report surveys (Wilson and Scior, 2014, p. 295). Among researchers, a popular way of measuring implicit prejudice is the Implicit Association Test, or IAT (Kassin et al., 2014, pp. 157-159; Wilson and Scior, 2014; Greenwald et al., 1998). Research has repeatedly shown that there is little to no correlation between measures of explicit prejudice and measures of implicit prejudice, and that the IAT is well-protected against faking (Banse, Seise, & Zerbes, 2001; Steffens, 2004). In other words, an individual may have little to no explicit prejudice, but a high level of implicit prejudice. Most importantly, the IAT reliably predicts discrimination—real actions which affect real people in the real-life settings (Kassin et al., 2014, pp. 157-159).

With the Implicit Association Test, implicit prejudice has been found in children as young as six and seven years old (Kassin et al., 2014, p. 158; Baron & Banaji, 2006; Dunham et al., 2008; Newheiser & Olson, 2012). Just as important as implicit racial prejudice is implicit gender prejudice, which also begins to operate in children from a very early age:

"In many hospitals, the newborn boy is immediately given a blue hat and the newborn girl a pink hat...Young children distinguish men from women well before their first birthday, identify themselves and others as boys or girls by 3 years of age, form gender-stereotypic beliefs and preferences about stories, toys, and other objects soon after that, and then use their simplified stereotypes in judging others and favoring their own gender over the other in intergroup situations (Golombok & Hines, 2002; Knobloch et al., 2005; Leinbach & Fagot, 1993; Ruble & Martin, 1998)... it is clear that children have ample opportunity to learn gender stereotypes and roles from their parents and other role models (Montañés et al., 2012; Tenenbaum & Leaper, 2002). Beliefs about males and females are so deeply ingrained that they influence the behavior of adults literally the moment a baby is born. In one fascinating study, the first-time parents of 15 girls and 15 boys were interviewed within 24 hours of the babies' births. There were no differences between the male and female newborns in height, weight, or other aspects of physical appearance. Yet the parents of girls rated their babies as softer, smaller, and more finely featured. The fathers of boys saw their sons as stronger, larger, more alert, and better coordinated (Rubin et al., 1974)." (Kassin et al., 2014, pp. 180-181)

Children are indoctrinated into a sociocultural milieu from the moment they are born. From the first moments of their life, infants selectively pay attention to the information they receive from from a native speaker of their language (Marno et al., 2016). Furthermore, children learn concepts even before they learn to speak: "a growing body of evidence documents that naming guides 9-month-old infants as they organize their visual experiences into categories", i.e., concepts which are taught to 9-month old infants via words shape the way infants experience the world and shape how they interpret their experiences (Havy and Waxman, 2016). The allegedly "biological" sex differences with "evolutionary roots" found by Western psychologists are just-so stories which legitimate existing social conditions and eternalize arbitrary cultural values. Much of this problem in contemporary psychology is a remnant of Freudian thinking, which treats objects as symbolic of genitalia; however, a stove is not inherently symbolic of a vagina (or castrated penis) and a car is not inherently symbolic of a penis. From the moment the sex of the child is established, shortly after birth, the parents and even the hospital staff (blue hat, pink hat) begin to project gender stereotypes onto infants and treat the infants as if these stereotypes were the truth; a self-fulfilling prophecy effect occurs, and the personalities of children are shaped by the overwhelming messages they receive from both cultural artifacts and the treatment they receive from others, especially their own parents. It is not only gender ideology which is acquired beginning from birth, but other ideologies as well: race, class, etc., viz. bourgeois ideology. As the Korean proverb goes, "What is learnt in the cradle is carried to the tomb."

It is not only the average person which suffers from implicit prejudice, but scientists as well. Evolutionary psychologists frequently tell just-so stories which legitimate culturally relative, socially constructed concepts as "science". That female scientists also engage in telling just-so stories is an example of the capacity of a person to engage in self-defeating behaviour due to the internalization of socially constructed roles, a phenomenon which is explored by the sociologist Pierre Bourdieu in his book *Masculine Domination* (2001). Western "evolutionary psychology" suffers from implicit prejudice, and is often at odds with the facts. Others have elsewhere provided lengthy criticisms of Western evolutionary psychology, in spite of which the ethnocentric speculations of evolutionary psychology make their way into textbooks and mass media. For criticisms of dominant opinions in evolutionary psychology, see: *Sexing the Brain* by Leslie Rogers (2002), *The Woman That Never Evolved* by Sarah Blaffer Hrdy (1999), *Social Bonding and Nurture Kinship* by Maximilian Holland (2012), *A Critique of the Study of Kinship* by David M. Schneider (1984), and

How Women Got Their Curves and Other Just-So Stories: Evolutionary Enigmas by Barash and Lipton (2009).

Our associations are stored, it must be remembered, in the cortex, which consists mostly of association cortex, where associations we have learnt are stored, like random-access-memory in a computer; and the information stored in the cortex, as Solms (2013) writes, tends towards automaticity, towards being implicitly active:

"It is of the outmost importance to note that in Friston's model prediction error (mediated by surprise), which increases incentive salience (and therefore consciousness) in perception and cognition, *is a bad thing* biologically speaking. The more veridical the brain's predictive model of the world, then the less surprise, the less salience, the less consciousness, the more *automaticity*, the better. One is reminded of Freud's "Nirvana principle," which he took to be the ultimate goal of mental life. The very purpose of the reality principle, which first gave rise to secondary-process (inhibited) cognition, is automaticity, *which obviates the need for consciousness* (it obviates the need for the subject to "feel its way" through situations)." (Solms, 2013, p. 14)

According to Friston's model, prediction errors, by causing more surprise and more consciousness, should be corrected and the "correct" idea should subsequently be automatized, replacing the false idea. However, in actuality, false ideas frequently remain uncorrected, and the cortex continues operating using automatized false ideas; the phenomenon of implicit prejudice proves that the cortex continues to operate using automatized false ideas *whether or not they correlate with objective reality*. Belief perseverance works at an unconscious level. Therefore, we cannot accept that the increase of incentive salience and the increase of surprise and consciousness are biologically "bad" and that the increase of automaticity is biologically "good". For an organism to effectively survive and reproduce, its thoughts (which guide its behaviour) must sufficiently correlate with the reality external to and independent of the organism. For an organism's model of reality to correlate with the objective world, the organism must increase its consciousness of the world and of itself—the more surprise the better, because more surprises means more opportunities to learn about the environment. Information in the cortex tends towards automaticity to reduce the cognitive load of working memory, not because automaticity is the "ultimate goal" or telos of mental life. More automaticity does not necessarily mean that the brain's model of the world is more veridical—to the contrary, more automaticity means that the organism is "running on auto-pilot", i.e., the organism is ignoring salient stimuli in the environment, which potentially poses a threat to the organism's survival.

For several reasons, there is no reality principle. Solms's reality principle in "The Conscious Id", which "obviates the need for consciousness", cannot exist because the less consciousness an organism has, the less aware it is of its environment (of reality), and thus it is in more danger. The ideology at work here is the same as that contained in the platitude "Ignorance is bliss": if the masses foster in themselves ignorance and a lack of awareness of their environment and the operations of objective reality, then they foster in themselves automatic submissiveness and obedience to social mores and to authority.

There are more fundamental objections that we have to the reality principle. As formulated by Freud, the reality principle is the function of the ego—the ego cognizes the reality external to the organism and thereby keeps the id and its pleasure principle in check like a dog on a leash. As we have discussed earlier, it is the drives and emotions which mediate the organism's relationship with reality, and reason is dependent upon the drives for effective functioning. However, another fundamental objection to the reality principle is that the organism—most especially human beings—does not have a sense of reality as such. As we have demonstrated by discussing implicit memory and implicit associations, the "reality" of the human psyche is often at odds with objective reality, and this is because what we consider to be "reality" consists of associations, of signs. We never experience the world independent of the mind. We only "know" the world through signs. All reality is virtual. We are forever interpreting signs.

In everyday life, we (our cortices) do not experience reality—our cortices produce reality:

"As a result, much of what we take for granted as "the way the world *is*"—as we *perceive* it—is in fact what we have *learned* about the world—as we *remember* it. This is best demonstrated by the fact that the way the world "is" can suddenly change—often dramatically—for people whose brains are damaged. As a result, and not surprisingly, some patients have great difficulty recognizing that it is them*selves* rather than the *world* that has changed." (Solms and Turnbull, 2002, p. 154)

Our memories of the world cannot come solely from individual experience; indeed, to what degree, if at all, individual experience is possible is debatable since we, from birth, live within a sociocultural milieu. The world as we remember it is also the world of our sociocultural milieu—it is the symbolic universe, the universe of symbols, into which we have been indoctrinated. The symbolic universe of a culture resides in the association cortex. The social construction of reality is achieved through the labour of the brain; the brain socially constructs, or produces, reality:

"The title of Gerarld Edelman's popular book, *The Remembered Present* (1989), captures very well what perception is about. We all automatically reconstruct the reality we perceive from models we have stored in our memories. We do not perceive the world anew every moment of the day and try afresh to discriminate recognizable objects and decipher meaningful words from the undifferentiated din of stimuli that constantly impinge on us...We adults [and children] *project* our expectations (the products of our previous experience) onto the world all the time, and in this way we largely *construct* rather than perceive (in any simple sense) the world around us." (Solms and Turnbull, 2002, p. 154)

The model of the world stored in our long term memory which we experience as reality is a virtual reality. Our brains produce, using socially acquired ideas, a virtual reality which we experience as *the* reality. The social production of reality occurs unconsciously—the social concepts which we acquired in early childhood are heavily consolidated and automatized into our long term memory, and have long since been active implicitly. The reality we experience in everyday life is a projection—the mind is a movie camera which projects a virtual reality upon consciousness, in which the self is both spectator and actor. Here the line between waking life and dreams blurs, for both are virtual realities generated by the brain's reality engine.

We inhabit a virtual reality nearly every moment of our lives:

"For a small infant, everything depends on the senses, and cognition is driven by concrete perceptual reality. During the course of development, however, deeply encoded and abstract knowledge derived from these early learning experiences comes to govern the perceptual processes. We therefore see what we expect to see, and we are either surprised or fail to notice when our expectations are contradicted. Experimental studies show that we frequently see things that are not there, simply because we expect them to be there. The best-known example of this is provided by the "blind spot", which is located in each eye at the point where the optic nerve enters the retina. For this reason, objectively, we have a hole in our vision (not far from the middle of the visual field) when we close one eye. Subjectively, however, this region is "filled in" with the texture, color, movement, and the like that are appropriate to what we *expect* to experience in that part of the visual field under prevailing circumstances." (Solms and Turnbull, 2002, pp. 155-156)

The deeply encoded and abstract knowledge which we derive from early learning experiences are social constructs, and these social constructs come to govern the perceptual process. We see what we are culturally indoctrinated to see, and when what we are taught is contradicted by perception, we fit the facts into the model, we reify reality, we appropriate reality, we legitimate the symbolic universe of our sociocultural milieu, and we maintain our symbolic universe through belief perseverance.

Our everyday life is an illusion, a dream. A dream produced by ideology, which follows us into our sleep. In dreams, our unconscious may have freedom of expression, but freedom of expression does not equal freedom of thought. Just as a society may have freedom of expression without sociopolitical freedom for its members—as we find, for example, in Britain and the United States, where institutional racism keeps minorities disproportionately in ghettoes and prisons—and where freedom of expression is in effect nullified by the constraints imposed upon thought by ideology, control is exerted even in dreams. The unconscious has freedom of expression in dreams, which means that it involuntarily produces the dream world without the interference and control of volitional consciousness—but the material and the machinery which the unconscious uses, its associations and ideas, are the social constructs with which it has been indoctrinated since birth. Control operates unconsciously, under the guise of freedom. To détournement Kierkegaard, "People demand freedom of speech as a compensation for the freedom of thought which they seldom use." Even in our dreams—perhaps especially in our dreams—we do not have sociopolitical freedom, we do not have freedom of thought.

The sociopolitical control exerted upon the mind in dreams is illustrated by the soliloquy of a dream-figure playing a ukulele in Richard Linklater's film *Waking Life* (2001):

"I had a friend once who told me that the worst mistake that you can make is to think you are alive, when you're really asleep in life's waiting room. The trick is to combine your waking rational abilities with the infinite possibilities of your dreams. 'Cause if you can do that you can do anything. Did you ever have a job that you hated? Worked really hard at? A long, hard day at work, finally you get to go home, get in bed, close your eyes, and immediately you wake up and realize that the whole day at work had been a dream? It's bad enough that you sell your waking life for...for minimum wage, but now they get your dreams for free."

The above soliloquy provides a concrete example of a dream controlled by bourgeois ideology—a dream of working a minimum wage job, complete with the quiet despair which accompanies it in waking life—but the control which ideology exerts upon our dreams is typically far more subtle, just as it is far more subtle in our waking life. The same implicit social constructs which generate the virtual reality, the illusory projection which we take to be reality, during waking life, also generate the virtual reality of the dream world, which is likewise an illusory projection which we take to be reality. In both virtual realities, these social constructs are embodied in people and objects—and in both dreams and waking life, the virtual reality may not correspond to objective reality.

Engels (1893/1968) wrote on the connection of *false consciousness* and ideology: "Ideology is a process accomplished by the so-called thinker. Consciously, it is true, but with a false consciousness. The real motive forces impelling him remain unknown to him; otherwise it simply would not be an ideological process. Hence he imagines false or apparent motives." Ideology is the symbolic universe in which false consciousness arises—the thoughts of false consciousness are false, even when the thinker believes himself to be free and honest. Ideology is not only conscious—it is also unconscious. A *false unconscious*, an association cortex storing automatized social constructs, produces a false consciousness. It is the false unconscious which makes us labour for corporations for free in our dreams.

The virtual realities produced by the false unconscious are the productions of our self, it's true, but it is also the dream of an other, an other which dwells inside of us, the other which is also the self, since the ideas and associations stored in our cortex have their origins outside of our minds—the false unconscious is a virus, a parasitic other. Thus, we should heed Deleuze's advice and beware of being caught in the dream of the other:

"Minnelli's big idea about dreams is that they most of all concern those who are not dreaming. The dream of those who are dreaming concerns those who are not dreaming. Why does it concern them? Because as soon as someone else dreams, there is danger. People's dreams are always all-consuming and threaten to devour us. What other people dream is very dangerous. Dreams are a terrifying will to power. Each of us is more or less a victim of other people's dreams. Even the most graceful young woman is a horrific ravager, not because of her soul, but because of her dreams. Beware of the dreams of others, because if you are caught in their dream, you are done for." (Deleuze, 2007, p. 318)

Lewis Carroll had the same idea in his novel *Through the Looking Glass* (1896/1993); Tweedledee and Tweedledum suggest to Alice that they may all be figures in the sleeping Red King's dream, and Alice despairs, not knowing whether or not she is real. Alice weeps, and thinks that her tears prove that she is real; she wipes her tears away, and turns the conversation towards another subject, but she still has doubts (Carroll, 1896/1993, pp. 201-202). Much later, in distress, she hopes to herself that she was dreaming— then immediately afterwards she adds that she hopes that the dream was hers and not the Red King's—she exclaims: "I don't like belonging to another person's dream..." (Carroll, 1896/1993, p. 241). But Alice is never certain whose dream it was; in the last pages of the novel, she is still troubled with the same doubts, and asks her kitten Dinah for an answer, but Dinah stubbornly remains mute (Carroll, 1896/1993, pp. 276-278). Whose dream was it?

It is with the dream of the other in mind, the dream of the other which we are already trapped in, that one possible interpretation of Cocteau's theory of dreams unfolds:

"I have said that my dreams were usually of the nature of caricatures. They accuse me. They inform me of what is irreparable in my nature. They underline organic imperfections I will not correct. I suspected these. The dream proves them to me by means of acts, apologues, speeches. It is not like this every time, unless I flatter myself, not having unravelled the meaning...The actions of a dream are not valid in a waking state, and the actions of the waking state are only valid in the dream because it has the digestive faculty of making them into excrement. In the world of sleep this excrement does not appear to us as such and its chemistry interests us, amuses us or terrifies us. But transposed into the waking state, which does not possess this digestive faculty, the actions of the dream would foul life for us and make it unbreathable...It is one thing to look for signs in [dreams] and another to allow the oil stain to spread over to the waking state and extend there." (Cocteau, 1946/1966)

But the oil stain of the other's dream has already spread over the folds of our waking life, it already threatens at any given moment to induce in our consciousness, if we are to become aware of it, a profound sense of nausea with all society and of the parasite within us. It is already the actions of the other's dream which we carry out in our waking state, and it is already the "digestive faculty" of the other's dream which makes our thoughts and actions excremental, *mediocre*—and it is the excrement of the other's dream which continues to amuse us and terrify us in our waking moments. We are already done for—condemned by birth within the bounds of civilization to live the foul life of the other's dream until death makes it unbreathable. We are already caught in the other's dream—we have been since birth—and freedom is only possible once we have escaped the dreams of the other.

References

- Abbott, B. P., Abbott, R., Abbott, T. D., Abernathy, M. R., Acernese, F., Ackley, K., ... Zweizig, J. (2016). Observation of gravitational waves from a binary black hole merger. *Physical Review Letters*, *116*(6), . doi:10.1103/physrevlett.116.061102
- Adler, R. B., & Proctor, R. F. (2014). *Looking Out Looking In* (14th ed.). Boston, MA: Wadsworth.
- Arendt, H. (2006). *Eichmann in Jerusalem: A Report on the Banality of Evil*. New York, NY: Penguin Books. [original work published in 1963]
- Aronsson, H. (2011). *On Sexual Imprinting in Humans* (Doctoral dissertation). Stockholm: Department of Zoology, Stockholm University
- Avalos, H. (2007, August 24). Creationists for Genocide. Retrieved September 29, 2016, from Talk Reason, http://www.talkreason.org/articles/Genocide.cfm
- Banse, R., Seise, J., & Zerbes, N. (2001). Implicit attitudes towards homosexuality: Reliability, validity and controllability of the IAT. *Experimental Psychology*, 48(2), 145–160.
- Barash, D. P., & Lipton, J. E. (2001). *The Myth of Monogamy: Fidelity and Infidelity in Animals and People*. New York: W.H.Freeman & Co.
- Barash, D. P., & Lipton, J. E. (2009). *How Women Got Their Curves and Other Just-So Stories: Evolutionary Enigmas*. New York: Columbia University Press.
- Baron, A. S., & Banaji, M. R. (2006). The development of implicit attitudes: Evidence of race evaluations from ages 6 and 10 and adulthood. *Psychological Science*, 17, 53–58.
- Bechara, A., Damasio, H., Damasio, A. R., & Lee, G. P. (1999). Different contributions of the human amygdala and ventromedial prefrontal cortex to decision-making. *Journal of Neuroscience*, 19, 5473–5481. (11)
- Belgers, M., Leenaars, M., Homberg, J. R., Ritskes-Hoitinga, M., Schellekens, A. F. A., & Hooijmans, C. R. (2016). Ibogaine and addiction in the animal model, a systematic

review and meta-analysis.*Translational Psychiatry*, 6(5), e826. doi:10.1038/tp.2016.71

- Bereczkei, T., Hegedus, G., & Hajnal, G. (2009). Facialmetric similarities mediate mate choice: Sexual imprinting on opposite-sex parents. *Proceedings of the Royal Society B: Biological Sciences*, *276*(1654), 91–98. doi:10.1098/rspb.2008.1021
- Bergen, D. L. (1996). *Twisted cross: The German Christian movement in the Third Reich*. United States: University of North Carolina Press.
- Berger, P. L., & Luckmann, T. A. (1967). *The Social Construction of Reality: A Treatise in the Sociology of Knowledge*. London: Penguin.
- Bhattacharya, R. (2002). Carvaka Fragments: A New Collection. *Journal of Indian Philosophy*, *30*(6), 597–640. doi:10.1023/A:1023569009490
- Blechschmidt, E. (1977). *The Beginnings of Human Life*. New York: Springer.
- Borrell, B. (2009). Oedipus wrecked: Study supporting the mother of all psychological complexes withdrawn. Retrieved September 30, 2016, from https://www.scientificamerican.com/article/oedipus-complex-study-withdrawn/
- Boag, S. (2006). Freudian dream theory, dream Bizarreness, and the disguise-censor controversy.*Neuropsychoanalysis*, 8(1), 5–16. doi:10.1080/15294145.2006.10773503
- Boagert, A. F. (2006). Toward a conceptual understanding of asexuality. *Review of General Psychology*, *10* (3), 241-250
- Bourdieu, P., & translated by Richard Nice (2001). *Masculine Domination*. Cambridge, UK: Polity Press.
- Bowlby, J. (1969). *Attachment and Loss V. 1: Attachment* (1st ed.). Basic Books.
- Braun, A. (1999). Commentary on "The New Neuropsychology of Sleep: Implications for Psychoanalysis." *Neuro-Psychoanalysis*, 1: 196–201.

- Brewin, C.R., Kleiner, J.S., Vasterling, J. J., & Field, A.P. (2007). Memory for emotionally neutral information in posttraumatic stress disorder: A meta-analytic investigation. *Journal of Abnormal Psychology, 116*, 448-463

- Buchanan, T.W. (2007). Retrieval of emotional memories. *Psychological Bulletin, 133*, 761-779.

- Carroll, L. (1993). *Alice's Adventures in Wonderland & Through The Looking-Glass.* Great Britain: Wordsworth Classics. [original work published in 1896]

- Chamberlain, H. S. S. (2006). *Foundations of the Nineteenth Century.* New York: Howard Fertig Pub. [original work published in 1899]

- Chalmers, D. J. (2010). *The Character of Consciousness.* New York, NY: Oxford University Press.

- Chivers, M. L., & Bailey, J.M. (2005). A sex difference in features that elicit genital response. *Biological Psychology, 70* (2), 115-120

- Chomsky, N. (2006). *Language and mind* (3rd ed.). Cambridge, United Kingdom: Cambridge University Press.

- Chuang Tzu, & translated by Burton Watson (1968). *The Complete Works of Chuang Tzu* (1st ed.). Columbia University Press.

- Cocteau, J., & translated by Margaret Crosland (2001). *The White Book [Le Livre Blanc].* City Lights Publishers. [original work published in 1923]

- Cocteau, J., & translated by Rosamond Lehmann (1957). *[Les Enfants Terribles] The Holy Terrors.* New York: New Directions Publishing. [original work published in 1929]

- Cocteau, J., & translated by Elizabeth Sprigge (1966). *The Difficulty of Being.* New York: Da Capo. [original work published in 1946]

- Cranefield, P. F. (1966). Freud and the "School of Helmholtz. " *Gesnerus, 23*: 35-39.

- Damasio, A. R. (1994). *Descartes' Error: Emotion, Reason, and the Human Brain.* New York, NY: Avon Books.

- Damasio, A. R. (1999). *The Feeling of What Happens: Body & Emotion in the Making of Consciousness*. New York, NY, United States: Houghton Mifflin Harcourt (HMH).
- Damasio, A. R. (2003). *Looking for Spinoza: Joy, Sorrow, and the Feeling Brain*. Orlando, FL: Harcourt Brace International.
- Damasio, A. R. (2010). *Self Comes to Mind: Constructing the Conscious Brain*. New York: Knopf Doubleday Publishing Group.
- Damon, W. (2015). Foreword. In *Handbook of Child Psychology and Developmental Science,* (7th edition). pp. vii-xiii. Hoboken, New Jersey: John Wiley & Sons.
- Darwin, C. R. (1877). A biographical sketch of an infant. *Mind, 2*, 285–294. doi:10.1093/mind/os-2.7.285
- Dawkins, R. (1989). *The Selfish Gene*. Cambridge: Cambridge University Press, 2nd edn.
- Dawkins, R. (2006). *The God Delusion*. Boston: Houghton Mifflin Company.
- De Benedictis, A., Duffau, H., Paradiso, B., Grandi, E., Balbi, S., Granieri, E., … Sarubbo, S. (2014). Anatomo-functional study of the temporo-parieto-occipital region: Dissection, tractographic and brain mapping evidence from a neurosurgical perspective. *Journal of Anatomy, 225*(2), 132–151. doi:10.1111/joa.12204
- Deleuze, G. (1992). Postscript on the Societies of Control. *October, 59*, 3–7. [original work published in 1990]
- Deleuze, G., Guattari, F., & translated by Robert Hurley, Mark Seem, and Helen R. Lane (1977). *Anti-Oedipus: Capitalism and Schizophrenia*. New York: Penguin Group. [original work published in 1972]
- Deleuze, G., Guattari, F., & translated by Brian Massumi (1987). *A Thousand Plateaus: Capitalism and Schizophrenia*. London: University of Minnesota Press. [original work published in 1980]
- Deleuze, G., Guattari, F., & translated by Janis Tomlinson and Graham Burchell (1994). *What Is Philosophy?* New York, NY: Columbia University Press. [Original work published in 1991]

- Deleuze, G., & translated by Ames Hodges and Mike Taormina (2007). *Two Regimes of Madness: Texts and Interviews 1975-1995*. New York: Semiotext(e).
- Derrida, J. (1998). *Resistances of Psychoanalysis*. Stanford, CA, United States: Stanford University Press.
- Descartes, R. (1968). . New York, NY: Penguin. [Original work published in 1637]
- Diamond, L.M. (2003). Was it a phase? Young women's relinquishment of lesbian/bisexual identities over a 5-year period. *Journal of Personality & Social Psychology, 84* (2), 352-364
- Dunham, Y., Baron, A. S., & Banaji, M. R. (2008). The development of implicit intergroup cognition. *Trends in Cognitive Sciences*, 12, 248–253.
- Dundes, A. (1980). *Interpreting Folklore*. Bloomington, IN: Indiana University Press.
- Fadok, J. P., Dickerson, T. M. K., & Palmiter, R. D. (2009). Dopamine is necessary for cue-dependent fear conditioning. *Journal of Neuroscience, 29*(36), 11089–11097. doi:10.1523/jneurosci.1616-09.2009
- Edelman, G. (1989). *The Remembered Present*. New York: Basic Books.
- Edser, S.J., & Shea, J.D. (2002). An exploratory investigation of bisexual men in monogamous, heterosexual marriages. *Journal of Bisexuality*, 2 (4), 5-29
- Ehrlich, P. R., Holm, R., & Parnell, D. (1963). *The Process of Evolution*. New York: McGraw-Hill.
- Ellenberger, H. F. (1970). *The Discovery of the Unconscious: The History and Evolution of Dynamic Psychiatry*. New York: New York, Basic Books [1970].
- Engels: Letter to Franz Mehring, (London 14 July 1893), translated by Donna Torr, in *Marx and Engels Correspondence* (1968), International Publishers.
- Eysenck, H. J. (1985). *Decline and Fall of the Freudian Empire* (2nd ed.). Harmondsworth, Middlesex, England: Viking.
- Faure, A., Reynolds, S. M., Richard, J. M., & Berridge, K. C. (2008). Mesolimbic Dopamine in desire and dread: Enabling

motivation to be generated by localized glutamate disruptions in nucleus accumbens. *Journal of Neuroscience, 28*(28), 7184–7192. doi:10.1523/jneurosci.4961-07.2008

- Feinstein, J. S., Buzza, C., Hurlemann, R., Follmer, R. L., Dahdaleh, N. S., Coryell, W. H., ... Wemmie, J. A. (2013). Fear and panic in humans with bilateral amygdala damage. *Nature Neuroscience, 16*(3), 270–272. doi:10.1038/nn.3323

- Fernandez, J. W. (1982). *Bwiti: An ethnography of the religious imagination in Africa.* United States: Princeton University Press.

- Field, T. M., Schanberg, S. M., Scafidi, F., Bauer, C. R., VegaLahr, N., Garcia, R., ... Kuhn, C. M. (1986). Tactile/kinesthetic stimulation effects on preterm neonates. *Pediatrics, 77*, 654–658.

- Freeman, W., & Watts, J.W. (1950). *Psychosurgery* (2nd ed.). Springfield, IL: Charles C. Thomas.

- Freedman, R., Lewis, D.A., Michels, R., Pine, D.S., Schultz, S.K., Tamminga, C.A., Gabbard, G.O., Gau, S.S., Javitt, D.C., Oquendo, M.A., et al. (2013). The initial field trials of DSM-5: new blooms and old thorns. *Am. J. Psychiatry, 170*, 1–5.

- Freud, S., & translated by Joyce Crick (1999). *The Interpretation of Dreams.* Oxford, England: Oxford University Press. [original work published in 1899]

- Freud, S. (1900). *The Interpretation of Dreams. S.E., 4 & 5*

- Freud, S. (1915) The unconscious. *S.E., 14*: 161.

- Freud, S. (1916–17). *Introductory Lectures on Psycho-Analysis. Standard Edition, 15 & 16.*

- Freud, S., & translated by James Strachey (1961). *Beyond the Pleasure Principle.* New York, NY: W.W. Norton & Company. [original work published in 1920]

- Freud, S., & translated by Joan Riviere (1960). *The Ego and the Id.* New York, NY: W.W. Norton and Company. [Original work published in 1923]

- Freud, S. (1924). "The Dissolution of the Oedipus Complex. *S.E., 19*: 172-179.

- Freud, S. (1926). *Inhibitions, Symptoms, and Anxieties. Standard Edition,* 20.
- Freud, S. & translated by James Strachey (1961). *Civilization and Its Discontents.* New York, NY: W.W. Norton & Company. [original work published in 1930]
- Freud, S. (1940). *An Outline of Psychoanalysis. Standard Edition,* 23: 144–207.
- Foucault, M., & translated by Jonathan Murphy (2006). *History of Madness.* New York: Routledge.
- Fukuyama, F. (1989). "The End of History?", *The National Interest*
- Galin, D. (1974). Implications for psychiatry of left and right cerebral specialization. *Archives of General Psychiatry, 31*(4), 572. doi:10.1001/archpsyc.1974.01760160110022
- Gilman, S. E., Rende, R., Boergers, J., Abrams, D. B., Buka, S. L., Clark, M. A., … Niaura, R. S. (2009). Parental smoking and adolescent smoking initiation: An intergenerational perspective on tobacco control. *Pediatrics, 123*(2), e274–e281. doi:10.1542/peds.2008-2251
- de Gobineau, A., & translated by Adrian Collins (1983). *The Inequality of Human Races* (2nd ed.). Torrance, Ca.: Noontide Press.
- Godelier, M. (2012). *The Metamorphoses of Kinship.* United Kingdom: Verso Books. [original work published in 2004]
- Goleman, D. (1990, March 6). As a Therapist, Freud Fell Short, Scholars Find. *The New York Times.* Retrieved from http://www.nytimes.com/1990/03/06/science/as-a-therapist-freud-fell-short-scholars-find.html?pagewanted=1
- Golombok, S., & Hines, M. (2002). Sex differences in social behavior. In P. K. Smith & C. H. Hart (Eds.), *Blackwell handbook of childhood social development* (pp. 117–136). Malden, MA: Blackwell.
- Goody, J. (2005). The Labyrinth of Kinship. *New Left Review, 36,* 127–139.
- Greenwald, A. G., & Banaji, M. R. (1995). Implicit social cognition: Attitudes, self-esteem, and stereotypes. *Journal of Personality and Social Psychology, 102,* 4-27.

- Greenwald, A. G., McGhee, D. E., & Schwartz, J. L. K. (1998). Measuring individual differences in implicit cognition: The implicit association test. *Journal of Personality and Social Psychology*, 74(6).. 1646-1480.
- Gregory, R.L. (ed.). (1987). "Plasticity in the Nervous System". In *The Oxford Companion to the Mind* (p. 623). Oxford: Oxford University Press.
- Guattari, F., & translated by Ian Pindar and Paul Sutton (2000). *The three ecologies*. New Brunswick, NJ: Athlone Press. [original work published in 1989]
- Guattari, F. (1996). *The Guattari Reader*. Cambridge, MA: Blackwell Publishers.
- Günther, H., & translated by G.C. Wheeler (1992). *The Racial Elements of European History*. Wayne, PA: Landpost.
- Hall, B. K. (1999). *Evolutionary Developmental Biology*. doi:10.1007/978-94-011-3961-8
- Hammack, P.L., & Cohler, B.J. (2009). *The story of sexual identity*. New York: Oxford University Press.
- Harlow, H. F., Zimmermann, R. R. (1959) "Affectional Responses in the Infant Monkey". *Science*, Vol 130, Aug, 421-432
- Havy, M., & Waxman, S. R. (2016). Naming influences 9-month-olds' identification of discrete categories along a perceptual continuum. *Cognition*, *156*, 41–51. doi:10.1016/j.cognition.2016.07.011
- Heard, E., & Martienssen, R. A. (2014). Transgenerational epigenetic inheritance: Myths and mechanisms. *Cell*, *157*(1), 95–109. doi:10.1016/j.cell.2014.02.045
- Hill, K. G., Hawkins, J. D., Catalano, R. F., Abbott, R. D., & Guo, J. (2005). Family influences on the risk of daily smoking initiation. *Journal of Adolescent Health*, *37*(3), 202–210. doi:10.1016/j.jadohealth.2004.08.014
- Hobson, J. A., & Pace-Schott, E. F. (1999). Response to commentaries. *Neuro-Psychoanalysis*, 1: 206–224.
- Hobson, A. J. (2002). *The Dream Drugstore: Chemically Altered States of Consciousness*. Cambridge, MA: Bradford Books.

- Hofer, M. A. (2014). The emerging synthesis of development and evolution: A new biology for psychoanalysis. *Neuropsychoanalysis, 16*(1), 3–22. doi:10.1080/15294145.2014.901022
- Hoffman, T. (2004). Revival of the death instinct: A view from contemporary biology. *Neuropsychoanalysis, 6*(1), 63–75. doi:10.1080/15294145.2004.10773441
- Holland, M. (2012). *Social Bonding and Nurture Kinship: Compatibility Between Cultural and Biological Approaches.* United States: Createspace.
- Holt, R.H. (2002). Metapsychology. In E. Erwin (Ed.), *The Freud Encyclopedia: Theory, Therapy, and Culture* (pp. 337-341). New York, NY: Routledge
- Hopkins, K., & Beard, M. (2006). *The Colosseum.* London: Profile Books.
- Howes, D. (Ed.). (1991). *The Varieties of Sensory Experience: A Sourcebook in the Anthropology of the Senses.* Toronto: University of Toronto Press.
- Hrdy, S. B. (1999). *The Woman That Never Evolved.* Cambridge, MA: Harvard University Press.
- Immelmann, K. (1972). Sexual and other long-term aspects of Imprinting in birds and other species. In *Advances in the Study of Behavior* (pp. 147–174). doi:10.1016/s0065-3454(08)60009-1
- Jethá, C., & Ryan, C. (2011). *Sex at Dawn: How We Mate, Why We Stray, and What It Means For Modern Relationships.* New York, NY: HarperCollins Publishers.
- Jirak, D., Menz, M. M., Buccino, G., Borghi, A. M., & Binkofski, F. (2010). Grasping Language – A Short Story on Embodiment. *Consciousness and Cognition, 19*(3), 711–720. doi:10.1016/j.concog.2010.06.020
- Kalat, J. W. (2016). *Biological Psychology* (12th ed.). Boston, MA: Cenage Learning.
- Kandel, D. B., Griesler, P. C., & Hu, M.-C. (2015). Intergenerational patterns of smoking and nicotine dependence among US adolescents. *American Journal of Public Health, 105*(11), e63–e72. doi:10.2105/ajph.2015.302775

- Kaplan-Solms, K., & Solms, M. (2000*). Clinical Studies in Neuro-Psychoanalysis: Introduction to a Depth Psychology*. London: Karnac.
- Kassin, S. M., Fein, S., & Markus, H. R. (2014). *Social psychology* (9th ed.). United States: Wadsworth Publishing Co.
- Kensinger, E.A. (2007). Negative emotion enhances memory accuracy: Behavioral and neuroimaging evidence. *Current Directions in Psychological Science, 16*, 213-218
- Kesey, K. (1963). *One Flew Over the Cuckoo's Nest*. United States: Perfection Learning Prebound.
- Kihlstrom, J. F. (2006). Trauma and memory revisited. In *Memory and Emotion* (pp. 259–291). doi:10.1002/9780470756232.ch12
- Kinsey, A.C., Pomeroy, W.B, & Martin, C.E. (1948). *Sexual behavior in the human male*. Philadelphia: W.B. Saunders.
- Kinsey, A.C., Pomeroy, W.B, Martin, C.E., & Gebhard, P.H. (1953). *Sexual behavior in the human female*. Philadelphia: W.B. Saunders.
- Knobloch, S., Callison, C., Chen, L., Fritzsche, A., & Zillmann, D. (2005). Children's sex-stereotyped self-socialization through selective exposure to entertainment: Cross-cultural experiments in Germany, China, and the United States. *Journal of Communication*, 55, 122–138.
- Konieczny, L., Roterman-Konieczna, I., & Spólnik, P. (2014). *Systems Biology: Functional Strategies of Living Organisms*. New York, NY, United States: Springer International Publishing.
- Lazarus, R.S. (1991). Progress on a cognitive-motivational-relational theory of emotion. *American Psychologist, 46*, 352-367.
- Leinbach, M. D., & Fagot, B. I. (1993). Categorical habituation to male and female faces: Gender schematic processing in infancy. *Infant Behavior and Development*, 16, 317–332.
- Lende, D. H., & Downey, G. (Eds.). (2012). *The Encultured Brain: An Introduction to Neuroanthropology*. Cambridge, MA: MIT Press.

- Levi-Montalcini, R. (1987). The nerve growth factor 35 years later. *Science*, 237, 1154–1162. (4)
- Lewis, W. C. (1965). ' "Coital movements in the first year of life".' *Int. J. Psycho-Anal.*, 46, 372-4.
- Linklater, R. (Director). (2001). *Waking Life.*
- Lippa, R., & Arad, S. (1997). The structure of sexual orientation and its relation to masculinity, femininity, and gender diagnosticity: Different for men and women. *Sex Roles, 37* (3-4), 187-208
- Mačiulaitis, R., Kontrimaviciute, V., Bressolle, F., & Briedis, V. (2008). Ibogaine, an anti-addictive drug: Pharmacology and time to go further in development. A narrative review. *Human & Experimental Toxicology, 27*(3), 181–194. doi:10.1177/0960327107087802
- Macmillan, M. (1997). *Freud Evaluated: The Completed Arc*. Cambridge: MIT Press. [Original work published in 1991]
- Mahabee-Gittens, E. M., Xiao, Y., Gordon, J. S., & Khoury, J. C. (2012). Continued importance of family factors in youth smoking behavior. *Nicotine & Tobacco Research, 14*(12), 1458–1466. doi:10.1093/ntr/nts078
- Majid, A., & Burenhult, N. (2014). Odors are expressible in language, as long as you speak the right language. *Cognition, 130*(2), 266–270. doi:10.1016/j.cognition.2013.11.004
- Malabou, C., & Translated by Sebastian Rand (2008). *What Should We Do With Our Brain?* United States: Fordham University Press. [original work published in 2004]
- Malinowski, B. (2001). *Sex and Repression in Savage Society* (2nd ed.). London: Taylor & Francis. [original work published in 1927]
- Marno, H., Guellai, B., Vidal, Y., Franzoi, J., Nespor, M., & Mehler, J. (2016). Infants' selectively pay attention to the information they receive from a native speaker of their language. *Frontiers in Psychology*, 7, . doi:10.3389/fpsyg.2016.01150
- Masson, J. M. (Ed.) (1985). *The Complete Letters of Sigmund Freud & Wilhelm Fliess, 1887–1904*. Cambridge: Belknap Press.

- Mayer, M. S. (1966). *They thought they were free: The Germans, 1933-45*. Chicago: University Of Chicago Press.
- Mayr, E. (2001). *What Evolution Is*. New York: Basic Books.
- Mays, D., Gilman, S. E., Rende, R., Luta, G., Tercyak, K. P., & Niaura, R. S. (2014). Parental smoking exposure and adolescent smoking trajectories. *Pediatrics, 133*(6), 983–991. doi:10.1542/peds.2013-3003
- McNamara, P. H. (2009). *The neuroscience of religious experience*. Cambridge: Cambridge University Press.
- Mead, M. (2001). *Coming of Age in Samoa: A Psychological Study of Primitive Youth for Western Civilisation*. New York: HarperCollins Publishers. [original work published in 1928]
- Mead,M. (1931). The primitive child. In C.Murchison (Ed.), *A handbook of child psychology*. Worcester, MA: Clark University Press.
- Merker, B. (2007). Consciousness without a cerebral cortex: A challenge for neuroscience and medicine. *Behavioral and Brain Sciences, 30*(01), . doi:10.1017/s0140525x07000891
- Mesulam, M. M. (2000). Behavioral neuroanatomy: Largescale networks, association cortex, frontal syndromes, the limbic system and hemispheric lateralization. In: *Principles of Behavioral and Cognitive Neurology* (2nd edition). New York: Oxford University Press, pp. 1–120.
- Mineau, A. (2004). *Operation Barbarossa: Ideology and Ethics Against Human Dignity*. Amsterdam: Editions Rodopi B.V.
- Moczek, A. P., Sears, K. E., Stollewerk, A., Wittkopp, P. J., Diggle, P., Dworkin, I., ... Extavour, C. G. (2015). The significance and scope of evolutionary developmental biology: A vision for the 21st century. *Evolution & Development, 17*(3), 198–219. doi:10.1111/ede.12125
- Montañés, P., de Lemus, S., Bohner, G., Megías, J. L., Moya, M., & Garcia-Retamero, R. (2012). Intergenerational transmission of benevolent sexism from mothers to daughters and its relation to daughters' academic performance and goals. *Sex Roles, 66*, 468–478.

- Morris, D. (2005). *The Naked Ape: A Zoologist's Study of the Human Animal*. London, England: Vintage. [original work published in 1967]
- Mosher, W.D., Chandra, A., & Jones, J. (2005). *Sexual behavior and selected health measures: Men and women 15-44 years of age, United States, 2002. Advance data from vital and health statistics.* Centers for Disease Control and Prevention. National Center for Health Statistics, No. 362.
- Moss, C. R. (2013). *The Myth of Persecution: How Early Christians Invented a Story of Martyrdom*. New York: HarperCollins Publishers.
- Myers, D. G., & Special Contributor C. Nathan DeWall (2014). *Exploring Psychology* (9th ed.). New York, NY: Worth Publishers.
- Nagel, T. (1974). What is it like to be a bat? *The Philosophical Review* LXXXIII, 4 (October 1974): 435-50
- Newheiser, A., & Olson, K. R. (2012). White and Black American children's implicit intergroup bias. *Journal of Experimental Social Psychology*, 48, 264–270.
- Nietzsche, F., & translated by H.L. Mencken (1920). *The Antichrist*. New York: Alfred A. Knopf. [original work published in 1881]
- Nietzsche, F., & translated by Michael A. Scarpitti (2013). *On the Genealogy of Morals: A Polemic*. London: Penguin Classics. [original work published in 1887]
- Nortje, G., Oladeji, B., Gureje, O., & Seedat, S. (2016). Effectiveness of traditional healers in treating mental disorders: A systematic review. *The Lancet Psychiatry*, *3*(2), 154–170. doi:10.1016/s2215-0366(15)00515-5
- Nyhart, L. K. (1995). *Biology Takes Form: Animal Morphology and the German Universities, 1800-1900*. Chicago, IL, United States: University of Chicago Press.
- Obholzer, K. (1982). *Wolfman: Conversations With Freud's Patient Sixty Years Later*. London: Routledge & Kegan Paul.
- Panksepp, J. (1998). *Affective Neuroscience: The Foundations of Human and Animal Emotions*. New York: Oxford University Press.

- Panksepp, J. (2010). Affective neuroscience of the emotional BrainMind: Evolutionary perspectives and implications for understanding depression. , *12*(4), . Retrieved from https://www.ncbi.nlm.nih.gov/pmc/articles/PMC3181986/

- Panksepp, J., Asma, S., Curran, G., Gabriel, R., & Greif, T. (2012). The Philosophical Implications of Affective Neuroscience. *Journal of Consciousness Studies, 19*(3-4), 6–48.

- Paus, T. (2001). Primate anterior cingulate cortex: Where motor control, drive and cognition interface. *Nature Reviews Neuroscience, 2*(6), 417–424. doi:10.1038/35077500

- Phayer, M. (2000). *The Catholic Church and the Holocaust, 1930-1965.* Bloomington, IN: Indiana University Press.

- Pigliucci, M., Murren, C. J., & Schlichting, C. D. (2006). Phenotypic plasticity and evolution by genetic assimilation. *Journal of Experimental Biology, 209*(12), 2362–2367. doi:10.1242/jeb.02070

- Pirsig, R. M. (1991). *Lila: An Inquiry Into Morals.* Bantam.

- Poe, E. A. (2014). *The Complete Tales & Poems of Edgar Allan Poe.* New York: Race Point Publishing.

- Popik, P., Layer, R. T., & Skolnick, P. (1994). The putative anti-addictive drug ibogaine is a competitive inhibitor of [3H]MK-801 binding to the NMDA receptor complex. *Psychopharmacology,114*(4), 672–674. doi:10.1007/bf02245000

- Prestwich, A., Kenworthy, J., Wilson, M., & Kwan-tat, N. (2008). Differential relations between two types of contact and implicit and explicit racial attitudes. *British Journal of Social Psychology*, 47(4), 575–588.

- Price, J. L. (2007). Definition of the orbital cortex in relation to specific connections with limbic and visceral structures and other cortical regions. *Annals of the New York Academy of Sciences, 1121*(1), 54–71. doi:10.1196/annals.1401.008

- Proust, M., & translated by C.K. Scott Moncrieff (2012). *In Search of Lost Time, Complete and Unabridged: Remembrance of Things Past, Volumes I-VI.* New York: Random House Publishing Group.

- Rathus, S. A., Nevid, J. S., & Fichner-Rathus, L. (2011). *Human Sexuality In A Diverse World* (8th ed.). Boston, MA: Allyn & Bacon.
- Reich, W. (1980). *The Mass Psychology of Fascism* (3rd ed.). New York: Farrar, Straus and Giroux.
- Reichard, U.H. (2003). Monogamy past and present. In U.H. Reichard and C. Boesch (eds.), *Monogamy: Mating Strategies and Partnerships in Birds, Humans and Other Mammals* (pp. 3-26). Cambridge, UK: Cambridge University Press
- Ring, T., Salkin, R. M., & La Boda, S. (Eds.). (1995). *International Dictionary of Historic Places: Volume 3: Southern Europe.* Fitzroy Dearborn Publishers.
- Rogers, L. (2002). *Sexing the Brain.* New York: Columbia University Press.
- Rohlf, J. W. (1994). *Modern physics from a to Z.* New York, NY: John Wiley and Sons.
- Roy, M., Shohamy, D., & Wager, T. D. (2012). Ventromedial prefrontal-subcortical systems and the generation of affective meaning. *Trends in Cognitive Sciences, 16*(3), 147–156. doi:10.1016/j.tics.2012.01.005
- Rubin, J. Z., Provenzano, F. J., & Luria, Z. (1974). The eye of the beholder: Parents' views on sex of newborns. *American Journal of Orthopsychiatry*, 44, 512–519.
- Ruble, D. N., & Martin, C. L. (1998). Gender development. In W. Damon & N. Eisenberg (Eds.), *Handbook of child psychology, 5th edition: Volume 3: Social, emotional, and personality development* (pp. 933–1016). Hoboken, NJ: Wiley.
- Rushworth, M. F. S., Behrens, T. E. J., Rudebeck, P. H., & Walton, M. E. (2007). Contrasting roles for cingulate and orbitofrontal cortex in decisions and social behaviour. *Trends in Cognitive Sciences,11*(4), 168–176. doi:10.1016/j.tics.2007.01.004
- Russell, B. (2004). *In Praise of Idleness and Other Essays.* New York, NY: Routledge. [original work published in 1935]

- Russell, B. (1945). *A History of Western Philosophy*. New York, NY: Simon and Schuster.
- San Roque, L., Kendrick, K. H., Norcliffe, E., Brown, P., Defina, R., Dingemanse, M., ... Majid, A. (2015). Vision verbs dominate in conversation across cultures, but the ranking of non-visual verbs varies. *Cognitive Linguistics, 26*(1), 31–60. doi:10.1515/cog-2014-0089
- Samuels, A. (1992). National psychology, national socialism, and analytical psychology. *Journal of Analytical Psychology, 37*(1), 3–28. doi:10.1111/j.1465-5922.1992.00003.x
- Sartre, J.-P., & translated by Hazel E. Barnes (1956). *Being and Nothingness: A Phenomenological Essay On Ontology*. New York, NY: Washington Square Press. [original work published in 1943]
- Savin-Williams, R.C., & Diamond, L.M. (2000). Sexual identity trajectories among sexual-minority youths: Gender comparisons. *Archives of Sexual Behavior, 29* (6), 607-627
- Savin-Williams, R.C. (2006). Who's gay? Does it matter? *Current Directions in Psychological Science, 15* (1), 40-44.
- Schneider, D. M. M. (1984). *A Critique of the Study of Kinship* (2nd ed.). Ann Arbor: The University of Michigan Press.
- Shapiro, L. (2007). The Embodied Cognition Research Programme. *Philosophy Compass, 2*(2), 338–346. doi:10.1111/j.1747-9991.2007.00064.x
- Sieberg, E., & Larson, C. (1971). *Dimensions of interpersonal response*. Paper presented at the meeting of the International Communication Association, Phoenix.
- Sieberg, E. (1976). Confirming and disconfirming communication in an organizational setting. In J. Owen, P. Page, & G. Zimmerman (Eds.), *Communication in organizations* (pp. 129–149). St. Paul, MN: West.
- Skinner, M. K. (2015). Environmental Epigenetics and a unified theory of the molecular aspects of evolution: A Neo-Lamarckian concept that facilitates Neo-Darwinian evolution. *Genome Biology and Evolution, 7*(5), 1296–1302. doi:10.1093/gbe/evv073

- Skolnick, N. J., Ackerman, S. H., Hofer, M. A., & Weiner, H. (1980). Vertical transmission of acquired ulcer susceptibility in the rat. *Science, 208*, 1161–1163. doi:10.1126/science.7189606

- Solms, M. (1999). Commentary on "The New Neuropsychology of Sleep: Implications for Psychoanalysis." *Neuro-Psychoanalysis*, 1: 183–195.

- Solms, M. (2000). Dreaming and REM sleep are controlled by different brain mechanisms. *Behavioral and Brain Sciences, 23*(6), 843–850. doi:10.1017/s0140525x00003988

- Solms, M., & Turnbull, O. (2002). *The Brain and the Inner World: An Introduction to the Neuroscience of Subjective Experience*. London: Karnac Books.

- Solms, M. (2013). The Conscious Id. *Neuropsychoanalysis, 15*(1), 5–19. doi:10.1080/15294145.2013.10773711

- Sowell, E. R., Thompson, P. M., Holmes, C. J., Jernigan, T. L., & Toga, A. W. (1999). In vivo evidence for post-adolescent brain maturation in frontal and striatal regions. *Nature Neuroscience*, 6, 309–315. (4)

- Spiro, M.E. (1965) *Children of the Kibbutz*. New York: Schocken Books.

- Stacey, J. (2009). Unhitching the horse from the carriage: love and marriage among the Mosuo. *Utah Law Review, 2009*(2), 287.

- Steffens, M. C. (2004). Is the Implicit Association Test immune to faking? *Experimental Psychology*, 51(3), 165–179.

- Stickgold, R., Hobson, J.A., Fosse, R., & Fosse, M. (2001). Sleep, Learning, and Dreams: Off-Line Memory Reprocessing. *Science, 294*(5544), 1052–1057. doi:10.1126/science.1063530

- Straus, M. A., Douglas, E. M., & Medeiros, R. A. (2014). *The Primordial Violence: Spanking Children, Psychological Development, Violence, and Crime*. New York: Routledge.

- Storms, M.D. (1980). Theories of sexual orientation. *Journal of Personality and Social Psychology, 38*, 783-792

- Sulloway, F. J. (1979). *Freud, Biologist of the Mind: Beyond the Psychoanalytic Legend.* New York: Basic Books.
- Sulloway, F. J. (1983). *Freud, Biologist of the Mind.* New York, NY: Basic Books, Inc.
- Symons, J., & Calvo, P. (2014). Computing with bodies: Morphology, function, and computational theory. In *Brain Theory* (pp. 91–106). doi:10.1057/9780230369580_6
- Taylor, A.J.P. (1967) Introduction. In *The Communist Manifesto.* pp. 7-47. London, England: Penguin.
- Tenenbaum, H. R., & Leaper, C. (2002). Are parents' gender schemas related to their children's gender-related cognitions? A meta-analysis. *Developmental Psychology*, 38, 615–630.
- Thompson, E.M., & Morgan, E.M. (2008). "Mostly straight" young women: Variations in sexual behavior and identity. *Developmental Psychology, 44* (1), 15-21
- Van Valen, L. (1973). "A new evolutionary law". *Evolutionary Theory.* 1: 1–30.
- Vos D.R. (1994) Sex Recognition in Zebra Finch Males Results from Early Experience. *Behaviour* 128(1/2), 1-14.28.
- Waddington, C. H. (1953). Genetic assimilation of an acquired character. *Evolution, 7*(2), 118–126. doi:10.2307/2405747
- Wang, X.-J., & Krystal, J. H. (2014). Computational psychiatry. *Neuron, 84*(3), 638–654. doi:10.1016/j.neuron.2014.10.018
- Webster, R. (1995). *Why Freud Was Wrong: Sin, Science and Psychoanalysis.* London: HarperCollins Publishers.
- Wierzbicka, A. (1999). *Emotions Across Languages and Cultures: Diversity and Universals.* Cambridge: Cambridge Univ. Press.
- Wilson, M. C., & Scior, K. (2014). Attitudes towards individuals with disabilities as measured by the implicit association test: A literature review. *Research in Developmental Disabilities, 35*(2), 294–321. doi:10.1016/j.ridd.2013.11.003
- Winecoff, A., Clithero, J. A., Carter, R. M., Bergman, S. R., Wang, L., & Huettel, S. A. (2013). Ventromedial Prefrontal cortex encodes emotional value. *Journal of*

Neuroscience, 33(27), 11032–11039. doi:10.1523/jneurosci.4317-12.2013

- Wiszewska, A., Pawlowski, B., & Boothroyd, L. (2007). Father–daughter relationship as a moderator of sexual imprinting: A facialmetric study. *Evolution and Human Behavior,* 28(4), 248–252. doi:10.1016/j.evolhumbehav.2007.02.006

Acknowledgements

This work was only possible due to: Gottfrid Svartholm, Fredrick Neij, and Peter Sunde (the founders of The Pirate Bay); Artem Vaulin (the alleged founder of Kickass Torrents); whoever the real founder of Kickass Torrents is; Kim Dotcom (founder of Megaupload); Alexandra Elbakyan (founder of Sci-Hub); the founders of Library Genesis; Google Books; public libraries; and other open access resources. This work was only possible due to open access; nearly all the sources I used were acquired through open access. Our minds will only be free when knowledge is free.

Appendix: Informal Self-Criticisms

If I were to revise the entirety of this work, my task would be endless; if I were to be even more consistent with my current philosophical views, I would have to throw it out altogether. All the scientific evidence and the inferences from the evidence which I present are accurate. However, the philosophy presented in this work is sloppy. I respect Descartes highly as a philosopher, and his work still remains highly pertinent today. The brain, after all, is an object which is contemplated by the mind; thus we arrive back at the mind, and no matter how much we try, we cannot prove that material reality exists. At the very least, let my modest work show that the ideas of Freud are wrong, especially when considered on a strictly scientific basis, which means that rejecting his ideas has nothing to do with "denial", and it has everything to do with acknowledging facts.

I have had the necessity to publish a second edition of this work because the original had a chapter on Carl Jung which was superfluous. In it, I quoted Bertrand Russell's *A History of Western Philosophy*, particularly passages in which, as other scholars have noted, Russell erroneously ties Hegel and Nietzsche with Nazi ideology. As much as I dislike Hegel, he is certainly not a Nazi; neither is Friedrich Nietzsche, as George Bataille and Walter Kaufmann both point out. Russell argues from indignation, but indignation alone does not make a reasonable argument. Also, oddly enough, Russell praises Heraclitus in the same book, and this is odd precisely because Nietzsche was a Heraclitean philosopher *par excellence*.

Heidegger, on the other hand, actually was a Nazi, at least in his political involvement; however much one may despise the man for his life, he was a much better philosopher than Bertrand Russell because Heidegger actually engaged with the history of Western philosophy in his works, whereas Russell was content with superficial and often erroneous analyses.

A few sources from the omitted chapter may be included, by accident, in the reference section, and I apologize to the reader for the inconvenience.

The original work was published on October 2, 2016.
—Irvine, California; February 25, 2017